Into the
Taylor-Verse

SWIFTIE

Into the Taylor-Verse

TAYLOR SWIFT'S SONGWRITING ERAS

Satu Hämeenaho-Fox

SIMON ELEMENT

New York   London   Toronto   Sydney   New Delhi

SIMON ELEMENT

An Imprint of Simon & Schuster, LLC
1230 Avenue of the Americas
New York, NY 10020

First Simon Element hardcover edition October 2024

SIMON ELEMENT is a trademark of Simon & Schuster, LLC

Simon & Schuster: Celebrating 100 Years of Publishing in 2024

For information about special discounts for bulk purchases, please contact Simon & Schuster Special Sales at 1-866-506-1949 or business@simonandschuster.com.

The Simon & Schuster Speakers Bureau can bring authors to your live event. For more information or to book an event, contact the Simon & Schuster Speakers Bureau at 1-866-248-3049 or visit our website at www.simonspeakers.com.

Manufactured in China

1 3 5 7 9 10 8 6 4 2

Library of Congress Cataloging-in-Publication Data

ISBN 978-1-6680-7053-6
ISBN 978-1-6680-7054-3 (ebook)

FOR THE SWIFTIES

Contents

Introduction

Taylor Swift's achievements are legendary. Although all the popstars have their own crowns, she has aced every test, winning fourteen Grammy Awards, forty American Music Awards, forty Billboard Music Awards, and twenty-three MTV Video Music Awards, and was named *TIME* Person of the Year for 2023. She is the most famous woman in the world. But as smart and hardworking as Taylor has been to win all these accolades, break so many sales records, and keep being so interesting we can't stop talking about her, there's something she does that is more important and more unique to her. She writes songs that mirror people's feelings so closely we joke that she wrote them just for us. Despite being a towering figure of fame, her music still feels intimate, like she's speaking directly to you. Although her songwriting has matured and become even more compelling, this emotional vulnerability hasn't changed since her debut album came out in 2006.

Long before the world knew her name, thirteen-year-old Taylor Alison Swift began her music journey on a New Jersey boardwalk in the summer of 2003. Wearing a butterfly T-shirt and an eager smile, Taylor performed a short set, including the first song she ever wrote, "Lucky You." Fast-forward to more than one hundred million album sales later, and that boardwalk has become the world's biggest stadiums. The T-shirt has been replaced with bespoke costumes, and the eagerness has been replaced with a powerful superstar aura. Little by little, Taylor curated an adult version of herself that still feels as friendly as the one in the butterfly top. She has created such an inviting universe within her songs, music videos, red carpet looks, and stage performances that die-hard fans (Swifties) spend hours at a time deciphering, studying, and trying to predict what she'll do next. There's a lot to discover once you step into the Taylor-Verse. It spans many horizons, from the rainy small town of *Fearless* to the midnight graveyard of *evermore*.

Starting from the early days as a small-town girl that inspired her debut album, *Taylor Swift*, this book explores the ins and outs of how Taylor writes her songs, one album at a time. We'll learn about her inspirations: muses who she loved and lost, her own girlhood, real people from history, and the work of William Shakespeare, to name a few. Taylor uses memory and time like no one else, especially to shape her songs about heartbreak. She is one of the world's greatest storytellers, using words, song structure, her personal life story, and her deep understanding of her fans to spin tales about everything from losing the love of your life to, well, shaking it off.

Taylor is not only a storyteller; she is also a mastermind. She has woven a whole web of connections between her songs and herself using the Easter eggs she plants from album to album, from important motifs in her lyrics to certain symbols and sounds, to meaningful color schemes and even hairstyles. On her tours, she leans into her innate theatricality to make her live show appear fun and effortless, although actually she's an all-star athlete doing an energetic three-and-a-half-hour show in heels. The Eras Tour, which the fans have made their own with costumes and friendship bracelet exchanges, has become a huge cultural event. As smart and forward-thinking as Taylor is, some of the most fascinating aspects of her career came when fate rolled the dice: when the political landscape changed underneath her; when public opinion flipped overnight; the Covid-19 pandemic. Taylor has had to grow beyond her image as America's ultimate good girl and become a more complex, resilient version of herself. Throughout the twists and turns of this journey, the Swifties have always remained dedicated, becoming integral contributors to the universe Taylor created. Taylor's relationship with her fans is the real stuff of legend: she listens, she notices, and she thinks hard about what to offer next.

Whether you're a brand-new fan or have been here a long time, put on your best dress and prepare to see the stars. It's time to travel into the Taylor-Verse.

1

Origin Story

TAYLOR SWIFT

*T*aylor Swift grew up in a small town. Like many a born star, she couldn't wait to get out and see the world beyond the mall and the Methodist church, the high school and the football field bleachers. Those early years have stayed with her, not just as memories of her childhood but in the first album she ever made, *Taylor Swift*. It's the only one of her albums not to have its own dedicated section of the Eras Tour, although most of the songs have appeared in the section where Taylor surprises the audience with tunes not on the permanent setlist. The themes and references Taylor uses in her debut album are expressed more simply than they will be in her mature songwriting, but this is still Taylor Swift. The scenes are set and the stories told in a way that lures people in like siren songs. Taylor wears little black dresses (and jeans—they never go out of style) with cowboy boots rather than high heels, and the stories are about the evergreen topic of yearning for love. Taylor will retell the formative experiences from her debut album in different ways: the hometown boyfriend with the Chevy truck in "'tis the damn season" (*evermore*) is straight out of

The scenes are set and the stories
told in a way that lures people
in like siren songs.

"Tim McGraw," while "Midnight Rain" (*Midnights*) tussles with the choice between a traditional life and the lure of fame. *Taylor Swift* takes us back to the summer when she made her decision.

Taylor Swift is interesting for Swiftian historians who want to learn her origin story, but it's also an astounding songwriting achievement in its own right. Taylor was just sixteen years old when her self-titled debut album came out. Like most teenagers, she paid close attention to the people around her, and her earliest stories were set in a world that looked very much like her hometown of Wyomissing, Pennsylvania (population 11,127 circa July 2022), or Hendersonville, where she went to high school (population 62,896 circa July 2022). By the time *Taylor Swift* was released, Taylor was a rising star in the world-famous music scene in Nashville (population 683,622 circa July 2022), a place known for respecting songwriting talent. Taylor had secured a record deal for songwriting at the ripe age of fourteen[1] and would never forget that it was her ability to tell stories and conjure up an imaginative world that helped her become a star. Her second most useful skill was her immense drive, which helped when she went on a radio tour, traveling the country introducing herself to producers, the people who decide which songs get radio play. Giving a great performance in front of a handful of grown-ups in a conference room isn't easy for any artist, but Taylor had a natural confidence that helped these important industry players warm to her, especially when she just kept coming back and treating them to new songs and another hour in her polite, smiling company.[2] They might have been standing in a conference room in downtown Nashville, but Taylor's music took them to an altogether different place.

On her debut album, Taylor takes us to an idyllic small town near a lake, where people drive pickup trucks and first love could potentially last forever—if the other person would just treat you right. The opening lines of the official first Taylor Swift song, "Tim McGraw," spirit us away to a starry night in Georgia. Your crush is gazing into your eyes and telling you how beautiful they are. Who wouldn't want to go to that place and never come back? Taylor creates a paradise of back roads and porches, safe and cozy, just like our earliest romantic daydreams. If this sounds like a hug of a song, Taylor thought so too. During her first tour, she would go into the crowd halfway through "Tim McGraw" to hug her fans and thank them for coming, before jumping back onstage to seamlessly finish singing about the poignancy of first love. The song is also a mission statement for the Taylor Swift songwriting process: she can write flowery comparisons just like any (tortured) poet, but she'll put a twist on them. The boy she likes compares her blue eyes to twinkling stars, just like Romeo does to Juliet in their famous balcony scene. But instead of indulging him, Taylor cuts him off, playfully calling him out for feeding her a line. Even though her debut album idealizes first romances and what could be, Taylor isn't going to fill her

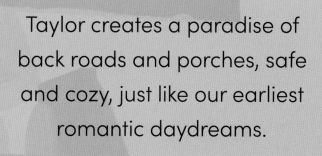

Taylor creates a paradise of back roads and porches, safe and cozy, just like our earliest romantic daydreams.

track list with songs bursting with grand, overblown metaphors about love. Instead, she will build a universe from the concrete, meaningful details that she remembers from her own experiences, from the little black dress she wears to dance with the boy in "Tim McGraw" to that scarf she'll later leave behind at someone's sister's house.

As first songs go, "Tim McGraw" is a perfect scene-setter for the themes of the album, and the entire career to come. It's about a real adolescent experience, but it's also about Taylor's bigger dream: to be recognized for her music. The song is full of metaphors that show Taylor yearns to be seen and heard for her lyrical talent. She doesn't just say that the moon and stars shine, she says they shine like a "spotlight." She doesn't just say "listen to me," she says one day you'll hear her on the radio. In fact, the word *radio* crops up on four of the songs on *Taylor Swift*, showing where Taylor's thoughts were leading. This choice of words reveals where she was at in her life. We'll discover throughout this book that Taylor's words have deep personal meaning to her, and also reveal her journey through life—Taylor was a teenager when she wrote *Taylor Swift*, so it's natural that the word *girl* features in five songs on the album; that was Taylor's world. Over time, the way she uses the word *girl* will change dramatically, particularly in her career-long struggle over the good girl versus the bad girl. Here, though, being a girl isn't complicated. If you're a girl, you're exactly where you're supposed to be by the logic of *Taylor Swift*—by the lake, with your crush, under the moonlight. The subtle genius of her word choice in "Tim McGraw" is that you don't have to want an actual spotlight to share in Taylor's yearning for it: we just want to feel special. The bright lights of fame are still to come for Taylor. Instead, this album is lit by the stars sprinkled throughout the lyrics. For now, she's a teenage girl, writing songs on her bedroom floor and hoping someone will like them.

Although the sound of *Taylor Swift* is organic, played on guitars and live drums, the story of how we came to know this record is a curiously digital one. A new technology came along at exactly the right time for someone who wanted to connect to others who felt like she did: social media. It's hard to imagine a time before it, but Taylor and social media were young together. Like any teenager at the time, she posted updates about her life, though her posts quickly evolved from her days at school to life on the tour bus, complete with period-accurate straightened hair and heavy-handed eyeliner (the YouTube makeup tutorial was yet to be invented). The stars aligned for Taylor to start her songwriting career at a time when culture was becoming less formal and glamorous, and starting to seek out more relatable stars. As well as shaking the hand of every producer in Nashville, Taylor hand-built her empire, girl by girl, via social media and in person. A fan named Holly Armstrong spoke to a podcast focusing on Taylor's earlier music, *The Swift Legacy*, in 2021.[3] She described how she watched Taylor play on a sandy boardwalk in Florida when she was twelve years old, and Taylor was thirteen. Taylor's set included a pre-*Taylor Swift* song called "Lucky You" and a cover of a song by country legend Patsy Cline. Afterward, Holly lined up with three other people to speak to this cool new singer. She and Taylor spoke about ordinary things, like their favorite color (purple) and their tops (Holly's said "American Girl" and Taylor's had a pink butterfly). By the end of their short chat, Holly felt like she'd made a friend and had been turned into a committed fan: "I don't think Taylor even really thought she was going to be as big as she is. You just don't think like that. You make the 'friend' connection with somebody and they play guitar, they do music, cool, I want to listen to their music." Holly was just one of the girls who Taylor turned her spotlight on, and who told their friends about this album of songs all about girls like them. They called up the radio station, on a landline phone, and requested her songs. And, using the new technology that had just recently become available, they went online (cue dial-up tone, because it's 2003) and commented on Taylor's MySpace, hoping she'd respond.

In the run-up to the release of *Taylor Swift*, methods of being a popstar were vastly different from today. When you saw your favorite singer, it was usually on TV or the front of a magazine, where they'd had the benefit of full glam; the interview was tempered by publicists and cut back by editors. In fact, a lot of gatekeepers stood between celebrities and fans, including the ones who ran the record industry and chose which lucky people would get a record deal. Navigating this forest of adult pressures is a lot to ask of a sixteen-year-old girl. Going from there being no such thing as social media to the existence of a site like MySpace was a giant leap in technology that Taylor was exactly the right age and disposition to take advantage of. Sarah Carson, writing in the *New Statesman* in 2021, looked back on the fervent days of her pre-*Fearless* Taylor Swift fandom, describing the appeal of a singer who wrote the swooniest music, set in a semi-mythical America, but also posted on the internet like a normal girl. One of Taylor's posts read: "I sit in class and write notes to my equally psychotic redheaded best friend."[4] MySpace Taylor even occasionally swore, something Albums Taylor wouldn't do until she snapped on *reputation*, showing that Taylor used social media just like every other girl at the time, testing the boundaries of how she expressed herself and letting her fans in on who she was when the grown-ups weren't around. Sarah wrote: "The music itself was only half the appeal [. . .] The other half was—and, for many fans, still is—the quest to understand her. We looked for hidden meanings in her lyrics, decoded the secret messages she hid in liner notes, and crafted in-jokes and fan theories."[5] These secret messages, whether they are actually in code or just left somewhere that only some people will notice them, have become an important way that Taylor speaks to her fans. She's created a perfect tension: between her inviting lyrics and warm personality, you feel like you know her as a person, but she sprinkles puzzles and mysteries throughout her work to engage your natural human urge to decode and decipher.

Taylor found her place in the world inside country music, but many of her early fans weren't exactly followers of a genre that was mostly aimed at their parents. It was Taylor who converted her fans to country music through the sheer power of her songs and personality. It's also likely that, growing up in Pennsylvania rather than one of the more typical country music states, she saw which elements work in the genre and cherry-picked them to suit her own purposes. A gifted storyteller like Taylor knows how to help listeners suspend our disbelief. To become a country singer, Taylor had to adopt a few Nashville-isms, like a twangy Southern accent, to really sell these songs about pickup trucks. Right from the start of her career, she understood that a persona is an important part of marketing her music, which is just another kind of storytelling. Her persona is woven all the way through her music and lyrics and was boiled down to the most compelling message on *Taylor Swift*: a wholesome girl whose world is still her tiny hometown, the next-door neighbors, and the street she lives on. Taylor would later say, "I think there's an interesting lag-time on emotional growth for me. Because I write my records a couple of years before I put them out, I've always seemed two or three years younger than I actually was."[6] Although Taylor was so young, she was still slightly older than many of her fans when *Taylor Swift* came out, and one or more years is a very long time when you're sixteen. One reason Taylor became a role model and "big sister" to many girls is the way she sang about her own immediate past with such tenderness and immediacy, while we also got to watch her life unfold on MySpace and Tumblr or, increasingly, in the headlines. The songs that would later become a multi-platform Swiftian universe baffled the other teenagers at Taylor's school, who heard her sing at talent shows and assemblies. The decision to write songs in a genre that wasn't exactly considered cool in the emo era of the early 2000s led to schoolmates telling her to "go sing that country beep" (Taylor's redaction).

Taylor's early experiences of being socially excluded at school (the first song she wrote for *Taylor Swift* was "The Outside," about loneliness) meant she looked for connection elsewhere. She says, "I had a double life. During the day I walked around, talked to people, went to class, studied for tests, and had crushes on boys, and then after school I would go downtown to Music Row in Nashville and I would write songs about those experiences."[7] Being cast out became fuel for her songwriting, something she would never quite get over, as evidenced by the loneliness present in every stage of the whistle-stop life story in "You're On Your Own, Kid" (*Midnights*). It also fueled her determination; she has talked about how she had the courage to approach record labels as a preteen:

"It's because I knew I could never feel the kind of rejection that I felt in middle school. Because in the music industry, if they're gonna say no to you, at least they're gonna be polite about it."[8] Other girls sensed that Taylor was keen to connect. By the time her first album came out, she was holding long meet-and-greet sessions, where she met and spoke to fans one-on-one for up to four hours at a time. When a fan asked for her signature, they'd often get a page of personalized notes hoping they enjoyed school this year and saying she would see them soon. Later, when her fans number in the millions, she won't be able to hug everyone or answer every email, but Taylor's interest in making personal connections never ends. These days she might drop a comment on an especially creative TikTok or send a care package to someone who set up a Taylor Swift Society at their college. It's even embedded in the way she sings—she's known for her direct vocal style that has almost no runs and frills, but instead feels like she's next to you, holding a conversation complete with sighs and laughs, something she will perfect and devastate us with in future albums. Then there are the Easter eggs that feel like coded messages only fans can read. What started in liner note codes ends with counting the number of birds in the background of her Instagram selfies for clues to the next rerecord.

We know Taylor has always welcomed her fans with open arms and continues to do so with each new album— whether it's brand-new material or a long-awaited re-release.

But why does her music itself create such a safe and cozy space? It should be obvious that an album by a teenage girl would come from a teenage perspective, but comparing Taylor's first album to those that inspired her, such as LeAnn Rimes's *Blue*, shows it's not necessarily the case. Young girls are often made to sing from a more mature perspective to expand their audience—*Blue* is full of references to loving your man and being a woman, which is strange to hear from a thirteen-year-old. Taylor took a different path, writing new, classic songs that sound perfect for people of any age to sing, whether you are still young or just remember that innocent time. *Taylor Swift* felt so welcoming to girls in particular because it's set in a world where girls make the rules. Even today, there are relatively few role models for girls; magazines for tweens often put Taylor, who is now in her thirties, on the cover as no one has come along to take her place. *Taylor Swift* is set in an innocent world devoid of the usual power imbalance. The lyrics of "Stay Beautiful" describe a neighborhood where girls lurk on corners, talking among themselves about whether a certain boy knows he's beautiful or not. It's a world where girls do the looking. The country music industry turned Taylor away at first because "girls don't listen to country music." It took her powerful artistic vision, and a seven-times-platinum debut record, to change their minds.

As well as having a distinct point of view, Taylor has another thing great artists often have: muses. On *Taylor*

Swift, these muses are almost exclusively boys, with one sweet song about friendship ("I'm Only Me When I'm With You," inspired by Taylor's best friend, Abigail) sneaking onto the deluxe edition. On the next album, *Fearless*, Taylor will still have Abigail for inspiration, and as time goes on, her muses will encompass romantic partners but also despised enemies and even the media in general. Muses have been part of the creative process of painters and poets throughout history—their beauty inspires the artist to capture a specific moment forever, such as when the boy in "Teardrops On My Guitar" glances at Taylor and she quickly smiles to cover up her feelings of unrequited love (good practice for keeping a straight face when journalists ask about her love life for the hundredth time). Over time, the media will become fixated on Taylor's muses and what the "real story" behind the songs is, when the most exciting part is how she turns all her muses into works of art. Taylor develops a playful approach to what listeners may have heard about her and her muse: in the *1989 (Taylor's Version)* track "Is It Over Now? (Taylor's Version) (From The Vault)," she references a tragic and widely disseminated 2013 photo of her looking extremely sad on a boat after a relationship-ending argument. It's not always easy being a muse, as some of them have learned all too well, but the compensation is that your uniqueness will be immortalized for all time. Taylor is not the only great artist to have written some of their most enduring works about having a crush

Over time, the media will
become fixated on Taylor's
muses and what the "real story"
behind the songs is, when the
most exciting part is how
she turns all her muses
into works of art.

on a cute boy; think of William Shakespeare's sonnets to his "Fair Youth." "Shall I Compare Thee To a Summer's Day" is almost as romantic and catchy as "Our Song." Shakespeare and Taylor both wrote from a place of yearning. While the crush holds the power in real life, the artist has the final say, something Taylor will emphasize over and over again, through claiming her rights both artistically as a songwriter and as the legal owner of her music. If she wants to talk about real events from her life, she will. She'll turn to her personal memories time and time again and start to analyze herself as well as the people around her, becoming her own muse on self-reflective songs like "Anti-Hero."

Taylor Swift captures the last moment before Taylor became famous. It crystallizes the worldview she grew up with, and which she'll spend her entire life and career building on. It's a simple world where love and family are all you need. On each album we'll learn more about Taylor and what her ideal love looks like, often through her relationship to home. The Taylor of "Mine" from *Speak Now*, written between the ages of eighteen and twenty, will treasure the drawer of personal items she keeps at her boyfriend's place. This domestic image of love will reoccur many times. Talking about writing *Lover* in 2019, Taylor said, "When young adults go from living in their family to then combining their life with someone else, that's actually like the most profound thing."[9] Building a home is at the heart of Taylor's concept of ideal love: the twenty-seven-year-old Taylor of *reputation* will share a home and chores with her partner; the thirty-year-old Taylor of *Lover* will build the whole damn house.

"Mary's Song (Oh My My My)" captures Taylor's ideal relationship at the age of fourteen. It's all about home, and staying there: two people meet as children, marry young, and spend their lives together in the same small town where they were born. Their childhood memories are shared; when the husband carries his new bride home, it's back to the house where they met as children. Even when they are seven and nine years old, their parents speculate about them falling in love. Written and delivered in such an old-fashioned, earnest way (and done so well), it boils the feminism right out of your brain. The teenage Taylor dreamed of finding love very early and being able to rely on it—an understandable goal. The quality of "Mary's Song (Oh My My My)" is able to sweep up the listener in a fantasy—even someone who has no desire to spend their life on a porch married to the first boy they ever laid eyes on. It is a sign that while Taylor's songwriting talent is built on relatability, she doesn't rely on it. At heart, she builds worlds and tells stories, and only asks that you suspend your disbelief long enough to really listen. She can take you anywhere; you just need to trust her.

Where is Taylor going next? To the top.

Shout-out Song

"OUR SONG"

The last track on *Taylor Swift* is the platonic ideal of a country song. It has plucky guitar, banjo, and fiddle, with Taylor and the boy she is seeing driving around the back roads (him in the driver's seat, of course). Country music values songwriting above all else, and it's known—or at least it used to be—for its wit. The concept of "Our Song" feels like it should have been already done a million times: a young couple doesn't yet have "their song," so they list out what it should sound like. Taylor lists perfect country music images: the sound of a screen door; of tapping on the glass of your girlfriend's window (an image straight out of *Dawson's Creek*); of her own laughter, which we don't get to hear just yet but will be an important feature on future albums. Some parts of their song are abstract, like his regret about not kissing her on the first date, or the way they talk in hushed voices on the telephone so their parents won't hear. And, finally, Taylor asking to hit "replay" and start the whole lovely experience again. In what will become a signature move, the final chorus flips their perspectives and has Taylor saying she could have been the one who kissed *him*.

Taylor's visuals, from her fashion to her music videos, have always been calibrated to add to her story. Trey Fanjoy, who directed the video for "Our Song," said, "We didn't want to do another boy-meets-girl story."[10] Instead, the video shows Taylor painting her nails and talking on a pink, old-fashioned telephone as if she's relaying the song's story to a friend. She then sings on a porch wearing a baby-blue prom dress with a skirt made of layers of fluffy tulle.[11] One day, in the video for "Look What You Made Me Do," Taylor will stand atop a funeral pyre of her old selves, and this "girly girl" in a baby-blue gown is the earliest version of herself that she will declare to be dead.[12]

If you think sixteen-year-olds in pretty dresses who sing about love are gentle sweethearts, you haven't tuned your ears into the bravado of "Our Song." Speaking about "the last great american dynasty" on *folklore*, Taylor will one day talk about using "that country music narrative device . . . in country music it's like [sings], 'This guy did this, then this woman did this, then they met and their kid was ME!'"[13] In "Our Song," after coming up with a perfect metaphor and writing it to a catchy tune, Taylor writes that she's listened to all existing music and there's nothing out there good enough to be their song. So, right at the end, as the music fades out, she leaves us with a mic-drop moment: that incredible song she's been talking about, that defines their relationship? Oh! It's this one.

I wanted ["Our Song"] to be last on the album, because the last line of the chorus is "play it again." Let's hope people take it as a hint to go ahead and play the album again.[14]

Into the Spotlight

2

FEARLESS

When the lights go out, the crowd screams in anticipation. Taylor is a blond blur as she headbangs like a rock star, standing in a wide-legged power stance. You can't hear a single note of her voice over ten thousand more voices singing along to every word. The crowd has listened to their *Fearless* CDs hundreds of times, memorizing every line. For the theatrical masterpiece "Love Story," Taylor rises on a platform wearing a wine-red-and-gold lace dress that would look perfect on an actor playing a princess at a Renaissance fair. She makes sure to sweep her eyes left and right, so no corner of the arena feels forgotten. Dancers in similar costumes twirl around her against a projection of a castle. For the song's triumphant ending, Taylor vanishes behind her dancers and then appears—*poof!*—in a white wedding dress, just one of many costume changes, including a marching band uniform and several sparkling minidresses in silver, gold, red, and purple. In the two years since her debut album was released, Taylor has learned how to transform.

Taylor toured constantly while promoting *Taylor Swift*. She learned about what worked from what got the biggest screams every night, from what girls wrote in breathless comments online, from the fan emails she tried her best to reply to. In writing *Fearless*, Taylor took everything that was so magical about her debut album—the intimacy, the honest emotion, the storytelling—and turned it up to 13. This is what helped her cement the loyalty of fans who had followed her since her "Tied Together With A Smile" days, and bring in new fans who were immediately addicted to upbeat hits like "You Belong With Me" and "Love Story." These are songs for singing in the car with your friends, or the stadium with ten thousand other fans. Taylor took an active interest in everything about the project of being Taylor Swift, from her stage sets (the fairy-tale castle) to what she wore in music videos, to the production choices on her album. This time, the production choices were a little less banjo. This caused some concern about whether Taylor was leaving country behind. If she was tempted, the success of the first single from *Fearless*, which opened with a delicately plucked banjo, proved that as long as she wrote her songs from the heart, she could triumph in the pop and country charts. Country music would keep Taylor for a little while yet, while the music industry at large was forced to take notice of "Love Story," despite it sounding completely out of step with all other contemporary pop

In writing *Fearless*, Taylor took everything that was so magical about her debut album—the intimacy, the honest emotion, the storytelling—and turned it up to 13.

(the biggest-selling single of 2008 in the US was "Low" by Flo Rida).

The hits helped Taylor do more of what she loved: connect with listeners. Once she drew people in with euphoric choruses, *Fearless*'s quieter moments turned out to have deeper emotions and more complex stories, capturing the essence of teenage life in tracks that were perfect for playing on repeat while crying under a blanket for reasons you can't quite explain. Being a teenager is like having the volume on your feelings turned up suddenly: they are loud and overwhelming. The music that describes this experience needs to be big and dramatic too, whether your preference is for thrill-seeking or looking out the window at the pouring rain that mirrors your soul. One of Taylor's enduring skills is to put a moment under a magnifying glass and express every facet of what she felt. For fans who had been through the same experiences as Taylor, these songs romanticized their own lives. For those who had yet to experience their first date or their first kiss, this was a beautifully rendered world full of promise, including the breakup songs: younger listeners already in the grip of the biggest emotions wanted to have their hearts broken so they could finally understand what Taylor was talking about in "Come In With The Rain" and "The Way I Loved You."

In the album's opening track, "Fearless," Taylor creates one of her signature atmospheric scene-setters, describing the rain-soaked sidewalk in such cinematic detail that it

One of Taylor's enduring skills is to put a moment under a magnifying glass and express every facet of what she felt.

feels like we're moving through the experience of a first kiss in slow motion. You can practically hear the rain falling, and the moment stretching out . . . until the chorus hits and Taylor is rushing into his arms (and the future). Taylor sings that she doesn't think anything could get better than this moment—okay, that's a wrap, guys; she's created maximum possible swooning. But after the romantic highs of "Fearless" come the demoralizing lows: the disappointments of "Forever & Always" and "You're Not Sorry" cut deeper than the irritation Taylor expressed for her cheating boyfriend back on *Taylor Swift*'s "Should've Said No" (when she played this on the Fearless Tour, rain came pouring down from the roof of the venue each night). The strings on "You're Not Sorry" in particular are mournful and dramatic enough to soundtrack the worst feeling it is possible to feel: teenage rejection.

One of the fears Taylor faces on *Fearless* is growing up and leaving the safe spaces of her childhood behind. On her debut album, she was afraid of leaving the warmth of her comfort zone and entering the hostile places she describes in "Cold As You" or "A Place In This World," where she's alone and no one seems to care. This sense of isolation in an emotional Antarctica will come back again and again in her songs, right up to "You're On Your Own, Kid" on *Midnights*, long after you'd expect her to be smugly enjoying success and surrounded by piles of invites to every party. The saving grace of being cold, though, is that it makes you feel alive; Taylor's greatest loves will also take her to upstate New York where the air is cold in "All Too Well," or get her to jump into the freezing waters of an outdoor pool in "Paper Rings." Her precious memory of swimming with her grandmother in "marjorie" (*evermore*) reminds us that memories stand out not because they are comfortable and cozy, but because they are intense. The shock of the cold in Taylor's songs is harsh, but it is also the essence of being alive. It's still hard for her to risk it by stepping out into the uncontrollable elements, the ferocious storms of teenage emotion, but she does it. An adult might look out of the window of their house and think, "This rainstorm looks like an emotional five at most," but if you're outside dancing in that rainstorm because you are fifteen and it's your first date ever and it's with a boy who has *a car*, it's a ten.

Lucky teenagers get to retreat to their family when things go wrong outside. "The Best Day" is Taylor's hymn to her family, particularly her mother, Andrea. In this song, when she gets cold, someone makes sure she's got her warm coat on (in its sister song on *Speak Now*, "Never Grow Up," Taylor will have to tuck herself in when her new apartment gets chilly). In "The Best Day," Taylor describes the social exclusion she went through at age thirteen. It is a formative experience that will shape aspects of her public image, and which she will return to over and over in song. The number 13 will also become Taylor's lucky number. She will write 13 on her hand from the Fearless Tour onward, hinting to fans how important it is to her, both personally and professionally. The number 13 will be sprinkled everywhere, from her use of 13 emojis to comment on fan posts, to the 13s and 26s iced on the wedding cake in the video for "I Bet You Think About Me (feat. Chris Stapleton) (Taylor's Version) (From The Vault)" in 2021. Just like with so many other heartbreaks, over time Taylor turned 13 into something positive she could share with her fans. But "The Best Day" is the only place she'll mention the number 13 in song (so far).

It's not necessarily easier facing life at eighteen. On the rainiest song on the album, the accusatory "Forever & Always," Taylor rakes back through her memories of a relationship that became so confusing she had to communicate with the guy via her *Saturday Night Live* monologue (something she wrote herself, impressing the writers at *SNL* with how fully formed it was—most hosts have their monologue written for them in the show's famous writers' room).[1] "Forever & Always" opens with the classic phrase "Once upon a time," just one of many fairy-tale references on *Fearless*, including Snow White in "The Best Day" and bonus track "Today Was A Fairytale." This latter song perfectly captures Taylor's grounded fairy-tale world: the love interest is a prince who wears not a silken frock coat but a gray T-shirt. Taylor delivers a twist on this theme with "White Horse," where she realizes that her belief in happy endings might be naive. It is about deciding to leave the small town that defined the world of her debut album and the local boys who seemed like such huge celebrities to her fourteen-year-old self. The biggest shock is discovering that the happy-ever-after of every story we consume in childhood just might not apply to everyone. "White Horse" reminds us that Taylor might be a dreamer, but she was never gullible. Think back to the very first lines of the very first song in her discography, "Tim McGraw": even in her most gentle, romantic fantasy she calls out the smooth-talking boy for feeding her a line about her blue eyes.

"White Horse" says you are better off heartbroken than unquestioningly staying where fate has put you. Remember Mary from "Mary's Song (Oh My My My)," who is fenced into her life path, not only by her future husband but by her own parents, who joke (not really) that she'll marry the boy next door, damning her with low expectations. Taylor was already testing the concept of happy endings, which she'll come to seriously doubt in the years ahead: "A fairy tale is an interesting concept. There's 'happily ever after' at the end, but that's not a part of our world. Everything is an ongoing storyline and you're always battling the complexities of life."[2] By the time she writes *1989*, her album all about fresh starts, she says, "I realized there's this idea of happily ever after which in real life doesn't happen. There's no riding off into the sunset, because the camera always keeps rolling in real life."[3]

The heart of storytelling isn't happy endings but conflict and tension. Taylor, a natural, picked up the need for conflict as well as happy, upbeat emotions from country musicians like The Chicks (formerly called The Dixie Chicks), and made the connection between storytelling tension and catchy music in the liner notes for *Red*: "I felt like my favorite writers have almost musical hooks in their work, whether it's poetry or a hook at the end of a chapter that makes you want to read the next one."[4] This must be why Taylor's music never feels overplayed. Okay, maybe if you worked in retail in 2008 you are entitled to a long break from "You Belong With Me." Taylor's intricate wordplay comes from the most 2000s musical genre, emo (she says Fall Out Boy influenced her songwriting "more than anyone else"),[5] and from hip-hop. Although Taylor might seem aesthetically far from Eminem, the biggest rapper in the world when *Taylor Swift* came out, or Lil Wayne, the king when *Fearless* was released, you could hardly be in music in the twenty-first century without being influenced by its most dominant genre. Taylor says the first rap song she ever memorized was "Fireman" by Lil Wayne, and she has covered Eminem's 2002 track "Lose Yourself" onstage.[6] Taylor's direct, speak-singing delivery and her frequent use of repeated single notes over more complex melodies has always been just a few steps sideways from true rap delivery—something she'll dip a toe into on "Shake It Off." Speaking of, Taylor can't have missed the previous generation's hip-hop-influenced pop singer Mariah Carey's own

2005 hit "Shake It Off," with trademark multisyllable words (Mariah's boyfriend lies "compulsively"—four syllables!) cleverly set to the beat. Taylor outdoes even Mariah with the five-syllable "absentmindedly" in "Fearless," rising to six syllables for "miscommunications" in *Speak Now*'s "The Story Of Us." Taylor may not sound like a traditional rapper, but she sometimes acts like one—her bravado is second to none. At the 2007 Academy of Country Music Awards, Taylor descended into the audience while singing "Tim McGraw," just as she did on her own tour, to serenade Tim McGraw himself; she ended by sticking out her hand to him and saying, "Hi, I'm Taylor." In 2024, when you think "Tim McGraw," do you even think of him? Taylor's instinct for scene-stealing and incredible self-possession helped her become the star she is today. That confidence extends to her music. Who is the one artist Taylor has sampled? Herself.[7]

Although *Fearless* is dreamy and glittering, it is also grounded in the real world of high school for two of its standout tracks. Taylor described walking into school on the first day of freshman year as scarier than walking out onstage in front of thousands of people. The cast of characters will be recognizable to anyone who grew up watching teen movies and shows, from *Gossip Girl* to *Riverdale*: adorable dorks, edgy outsiders, queen bees. "You Belong With Me" invokes the most powerful and yet darkest figure in all of girl culture: the mean girl. Taylor knows that her audience will understand the significance of a cheer captain, who she contrasts, still convincingly in this era, with herself as a "loser" who wears sneakers and never gets the guy. Taylor will eventually take on every quality she attributes to her crush's girlfriend, from the short skirts to the screaming on the phone ("*Je suis calme!*"). It's not Taylor's job to present the calm, considered take on a situation; it's her job to capture our attention with relatable sentiments, one of which is jealousy. But given that in the "You Belong With Me" video she puts on a brunette wig and plays her own love rival, Taylor knows that we all can play both parts in different people's eyes: the nice, chosen love interest in the white gown, or the supposedly mean girl in the red cutout dress. In her *1989* era, Taylor will present herself as the cheerleader, the de facto queen of the school, in a way that gradually becomes less tongue-in-cheek as she commits to becoming one of the "cool girls" she laughed at and maybe secretly envied when she was a teenager. Using female archetypes borrowed from American twentieth-century mythology, like the cheerleader and the bride, helped Taylor keep her messaging concise. As time goes on, and Taylor comes to understand the tiny boxes women are allowed to inhabit, she'll get more restless about being confined to stereotypes. On *folklore* she'll be a "mad woman," and on *Midnights* she'll be a monster in "Anti-Hero." But for now, she's an ordinary teenage girl who must figure out what the boxes even are before she can break out of them.

In "Fifteen," her magnificent document of the intense, transformative period of that year, Taylor nails how a

It's not Taylor's job to present
the calm, considered take on a
situation; it's her job to capture
our attention with relatable
sentiments, one of which
is jealousy.

teenage girl can be at once shy and vulnerable (blushing when a cute guy winks at her) and full of bravado (thinking you know everything, MOM). There is even the first implication of sex in Taylor's music, in the story of her best friend, Abigail, who was let down by a boy to whom she gave "everything." At just eighteen, Taylor was already looking back on her teenage experiences with compassion, as if they had happened in the distant past. These experiences have become part of her personal mythology through her writing them into songs, and then hearing them sung back to her by thousands of people. Listening to Taylor's early work is like listening to a myth being written, live. The song's power is brought out even more in "Fifteen (Taylor's Version)." Hearing an adult Taylor—a woman who has achieved unimaginable professional success, expressed herself artistically at a genius level, and immeasurably brightened up the lives of millions of people—reflect that she'll achieve more in her life

Taylor was already looking back on her teenage experiences with compassion, as if they had happened in the distant past.

than dating some guy, is immensely poignant. We could all have used that advice at fifteen, if only we'd been willing to hear it. Life can be scary, out from under the blanket and beyond the rain-soaked window. But that's what growing up is all about in the Taylor-Verse: feeling the fear and dancing anyway.

On paper, this song has no right to go this hard. It rewrites the ultimate love story, *Romeo and Juliet*, and removes what has made that story resonate across the centuries: its ending. "Love Story" throws out the tragedy but keeps the high drama. It's pitch-perfect. No reference to princesses or ball gowns or Shakespeare could ever be *too much* when you are the one in love.

Taylor's songs are so often about memory—she says, "All we have are our memories, and our hope for future memories. I just like to hopefully give people a soundtrack to those things."[8] "Love Story" has a framing device straight out of classic literature: an older Juliet remembering when she first saw Romeo, when they were young. But the path of true love does not run smooth: Juliet's father forbids them from being together. This was apparently inspired by Taylor's father, Scott, who does not seem like the type to wave a shotgun around but wasn't sure if he liked her new love interest at the time.[9] Taylor stomped off to her room and wrote the song in twenty minutes.[10]

Taylor took inspiration from "crush stuff that had happened in my life," along with romantic movies and, of course, Shakespeare. Explaining the small, ordinary drama of a girl who wants to be with a boy, she said, "As a writer you try to expand moments. You try to take a micro emotion or a feeling you had for two minutes in the day and you take that and you zoom into it and you try to explore it."[11] Taylor zooms in close to her character, Juliet, tracking her every movement and emotion, from the moment she steps into the ball, to the speech she makes to Romeo somewhere on the edge of town, a fringe location where the reliable rules of small-town life have become unclear. What if this love story doesn't end with marriage? Just like in (Shakespeare's Version), the villain in this story is a lack of communication. But this time Taylor is the playwright and what she says goes: "I added the ending 'cause I want that ending [. . .] That's the girly girl in me."[12]

In the best part of any song ever, the tension cranks up as a confused Juliet appeals to Romeo for answers. Even though this situation is difficult, is their love real? It feels like all of girlhood is there in that moment, the feeling of waiting for life to begin. Juliet, and the music, is fizzing like a shaken champagne bottle. At last, the key changes and so does Juliet's life. He does want her! Romeo is the ultimate modern hero: he soothes the angry father, and even makes the wedding arrangements—all Juliet has to do is choose a dress.

There is something timeless about "Love Story." Taylor's process of rerecording her first six albums has increased scrutiny of her earlier albums. Songs like "Fifteen" sound more poignant, while "You Belong With Me" and "Better Than Revenge," for all their titanium-strong songcraft, don't chime with the Taylor we know today. "Love Story" could

The lyrics of "Love Story" are
still the most searched-for
online out of Taylor's whole
back catalog.

have been written yesterday. It is about falling in love and getting married, but it could really be about any scenario where you have invested all of yourself into a dream that you fear might slip away; Romeo is "everything" to Juliet, in typical all-or-nothing teenage style. That black-and-white passion is this song's core. Every fan in every demographic likes this song, from kids to dads. Maybe you fell in love with it in 2008 because it hit just as you were experiencing the tentative steps of early love for the first time, and you really felt like you had something to lose. Or perhaps you are one of those who heard it on restaurant drama *The Bear* and discovered its incredible fist-pumping energy. Getting down on one knee to scream-sing this song is an appropriate response no matter where you encounter it: all these years later, the lyrics of "Love Story" are still the most searched-for online out of Taylor's whole back catalog. Those sparkling opening notes on the banjo now signify so much more than Taylor staying country: it's the sound of pure romance, of nervous anticipation, and of triumphing despite the odds.

3

The Final
Fairy Tale

SPEAK NOW

*T*he first three albums of Taylor's career—*Taylor Swift*, *Fearless*, and *Speak Now*—were written while she was being forged in the fires of teenagerhood, turned from an ordinary kid into sparkly, superstar material. Taylor has always been closely associated with girlhood and she'll never lose that playful, innocent part of her. But girlhood must end, often in flames. Far in the future, on *Midnights*, Taylor will write a song about the ending of her girlhood called "Would've, Could've, Should've," and it will reach back to put its arms around the Taylor of "Dear John." It knows she's going through girlhood's Ragnarök, releasing her old beliefs so that the woman can emerge. It is inevitable but devastating (shall we just go back to *Fearless* and pretend none of this is happening?). Reflecting on the writing of *Speak Now* as she prepared to release the rerecorded version in 2023, Taylor described the years between eighteen and twenty as "vibrantly aglow with the last light of the setting sun of my childhood."[1] She held on to girlhood for herself, and for us, for one more album.

Taylor's previous album, *Fearless*, was all about the desire to be transformed by love's magic wand, and the difficulties of getting the rest of the world to treat you like a fairy-tale princess, or just as a person. Taylor had to weather a growing flurry of criticisms, ranging from the strength of her voice to setting a bad example for kids.[2] In order to stay in control, she had to create her own castle, casting herself as the damsel in her songs and videos, while also casting cute, charming boys as her love interests (who among us?). By "Long Live," the final track of *Speak Now*, Taylor was done being a princess. The song doubles as her own statement for adult life: she describes herself and her friends as "kings and queens" stepping into an unknown future. From then on, Taylor portrays herself as a woman ruler—listen for her calling herself a "queen" in songs like "Blank Space" and "King Of My Heart." On the *Speak Now* track "Castles Crumbling (feat. Hayley Williams) (Taylor's Version) (From The Vault)," she even considers herself the ruler of an empire, although one constantly in peril of collapse. It is majestic to hear her beginning to own her power. Over ten years later, it will be even more incredible to hear her calling out the man who destroyed her sense of self in "Would've, Could've, Should've." This painful, powerful song is all the more poignant given that she created such an enchanting portrait of her girlhood in her music.

Taylor was twenty-one when *Speak Now* was released, and, instead of college, she was graduating from the university of public opinion, with qualifications in winning Grammys. The ages fifteen to nineteen are referenced more in Taylor's songs than every other age put together. In her words, the late teens are the "most emotionally turbulent" but also "the most idealistic and hopeful" time in a person's life, both of which are captured on *Speak Now*, which introduces new ways of being Taylor.[3] There's a hint of Taylor the celebrity, but she doesn't write songs about how awful it is being famous: "I wanted one thing [my] whole life. . . . I'm not going to get it and then complain about it."[4] *Fearless* had a curious double existence. It was the biggest-selling album of the year in America. It won the Grammy for Album of the Year, and although these awards' reputation has steadily decreased over the years, with one baffling exclusion after another (justice for Beyoncé), Taylor cares about the Grammys and therefore so do her fans. The Grammys are voted for by musicians and industry people, and it is natural to want that acceptance from those you work with. In fact, acceptance is all any teenager wants. A teenager who wrote all about being "Invisible" and on "The Outside" on her debut album would be levitating with pride if she was handed the most golden of gold stars for a perfect grade.

But although *Fearless* was loved by the many, *many* people who bought it in the first week alone— Wait, we need to pause here and really linger on those *Fearless* sales figures. In 2008, the overall number of albums sold in America fell from 500 million to just 428 million, a sign that the music industry needed to worry about where its next $100 million was coming from.[5] Taylor bucked the trend, selling 4 million copies of *Fearless* in a year. The album was loved by both its target audience and relieved and impressed Grammy voters who needed the music industry to keep profiting. As Taylor's star rose, more people noticed that a teenage girl was being lauded as the next great thing in music, and that couldn't be right. Although "rockist" criticism that only endorsed guitar music made by men singing about drinking whiskey across the state line was gradually softening and being replaced by a more "poptimist" approach that saw the value in a broader range of music, there was still plenty of baseless snark to go around in 2008.

Reviews started to comment on Taylor's singing voice, with headlines like "Hey, Has Anybody Noticed That Taylor Swift Can't Sing?"[6] Taylor was irritated by escalating skepticism about her talent after her historic Grammy win (she was the youngest artist to win Album of the Year, until Billie Eilish won in 2020): "All of a sudden people had doubts about my singing voice [. . .] they weren't sure if I was the one writing the songs because sometimes in the past I had had cowriters in the room."[7] Taylor reacted with characteristic studiousness: she took singing lessons and worried about whether she was going to lose everything she'd worked so hard for.

Taylor's voice is stronger than some critics have given her credit for. It is not the skill that got her the record deal, but there is a hard truth that people ignore: being a really good singer doesn't make you a popstar. In fact, the "best" singer on a stage is often one of the backing vocalists.[8] Being able to interpret and sell a song to the listener is everything in pop, which is why singers with a unique tone and an ability to tell a story are the most beloved of all time, from Bob Dylan to Britney Spears. Shaming singers for human mistakes is what led to Auto-Tune being rolled out so widely, resulting in a robotic-ness to modern vocals that you barely notice unless you go back and listen to singers from the nineties and before (treasure the off-key quavers of a vintage vocal). Having said this, Taylor is a good singer. She has an advantage in delivering her own songs beautifully because she wrote them for her vocal range and strengths, such as her talent for spitting complex sequences of lyrics or delivering words in almost a whisper. Taylor described how "your [own] songs are easy . . . you find that place in your voice where you're not pushing, you're just floating."[9] Even stellar singers like Kelly Clarkson find covering Taylor's songs a medium-size challenge. Kelly's version of "Clean" is lovely, although as a high soprano she struggles to hit Taylor's earthy lower notes; her "Delicate" is even trickier because the song has an insistent, repeated line that leaves nowhere to hide. Do not choose "Delicate," "Out Of The Woods," or "Lover" for karaoke! You'll doubt yourself as you approach the fourth identical "my" in "Lover" and you will crumble. That's when you'll understand Taylor's strength as a singer, and how she commits to her performances.

Nettled by the rockist commentary around *Fearless*, Taylor made a point of writing every song on *Speak Now* alone, as well as producing and contributing many of her own vocal harmonies. On her debut album, Taylor had written three songs on her own, including the standout "Our Song," and collaborated with the brilliant Nashville songwriter Liz Rose on many others. On *Fearless*, it was seven songs, including "Love Story." To this day, Taylor keeps dropping one solo song per album, just to remind us that she can: "my tears ricochet," "no body, no crime (feat. HAIM)," and "Vigilante Shit" are all credited only to Taylor. Some of the songs on *Speak Now* are perfect versions of concepts she'd explored before: "Sparks Fly" is a romantic song about the kinetic energy of falling in love, just like "Fearless." "Mine" is simply a masterwork of lyrics fitted together like a puzzle box made by a clever woodworker. In fact, *Speak Now* as an album is a masterpiece in the old-fashioned sense: the perfect example of a craftsperson's work, presented to prove they are a fully fledged artisan. Not necessarily the greatest work they'll ever do—that could still be to come—but the one that proves they have reached maturity. Taylor's membership of the ancient guild of authentic songwriters was proved by *Speak Now*, plus she graduated from playing arenas to stadiums, the ultimate sign of having made it as a superstar artist. As well as proving her point, writing her own songs meant that Taylor leaned into her own instincts for how to structure them. The songs stretched out longer and included a new element only hinted at on *Fearless*. It's the place in the song where listeners live, cry, die, and come back to life. It's the all-important Swiftian bridge.

You notice it first on "Back To December." The song is already new territory for Taylor, as she's acknowledging her own mistakes for the first time. She's the one who broke someone else's heart, and, after so many songs of wishing someone would knock on her door, Taylor is the one at his door, coming back to ask for another chance. Just when you think you know what this song's deal is, at three minutes and eight seconds in, she takes it up a notch in an impassioned bridge that ends in resignation and regret (this is on my personal cry playlist). Four full minutes into the slow-burn tour de force of toxic relationship dynamics, gaslighting, and bitter disappointment that is "Dear John," Taylor moves out of the resigned register she began in to spit out the bridge in a cry of pain. She snarls a list of the titular John's skills of emotional manipulation, such as constantly changing the rules for how to please him. This has the awful side effect of making Taylor fixate on trying to solve the puzzle that is this man. Eventually, she does the only thing she can do, which is flee, leaving his calls unanswered. There has been much speculation about who "Dear John" is about, and whether it's okay for Taylor to include someone's name in her song titles. It's tough: Taylor has such a big platform, and such a compelling ability to express her emotions, that telling her own story can lead to unintended consequences, with huge numbers of nasty comments flung at her suspected exes. For many years, she stopped playing "Dear John" at her concerts, and when she finally brought it back after eleven years on the Eras Tour, she told fans clearly that this was not an encouragement to attack any individual: "I'm not putting [*Speak Now (Taylor's Version)*] out so that you could go and, like, feel the need to defend me on the internet against someone you think I might have written a song about fourteen billion years ago."[10] It's natural to have curiosity about fellow celebrities Taylor might have dated, but this could be John who works at the Wyomissing gas station and the song would have the same power. Taylor's songs are about her life, but they became about ours. A document signed by Taylor telling us who each of her songs is about wouldn't change the fact that they feel like she wrote them for us, about our actual lives (how did she *know*?). As Taylor wrote on releasing the rerecorded version of *Speak Now* in 2023, "It's yours, it's mine, it's ours."[11]

All the best bridges on this album are on the sad songs, and it doesn't get more cry playlist than "Last Kiss." This song has the kind of deceptively simple melody that feels like it has always existed. The gently insistent rhythm is reminiscent of waves of rain on the window as Taylor collapses on the floor, remembering her ex's broken promise

Taylor's songs are about her life,
but they became about ours.

to love her forever. The downpour is a callback to "Fearless," when the weather sets the scene of a glorious first kiss; "Last Kiss" is the end of that story. When she plays it on tour, Taylor accurately says, "It's time to play 'Last Kiss' and cry."[12] As a portrait of a relationship, it does so much with few words: the ex is a show-off and a party animal, someone who rudely interrupts Taylor when she's trying to speak, and she loved him because of this, not in spite of it. This song has so many early Taylor-isms, like the late hour (1:58 a.m.), the rain-soaked pavement, and introducing someone to her dad. It's time to say goodbye to some of these things: Taylor's dad gets one more moment in the sun on "All Too Well (10 Minute Version) (Taylor's Version) (From The Vault)," and while there'll always be rain and late nights, they'll never be ubiquitous again. *Fearless* had five songs that mentioned rain, *Speak Now* three. Taylor has firmly established romantic rain as one of her magic symbols and, from now on, she'll use it sparingly, trusting us to recognize it as a callback to this tender, deeply romantic reference point. Rain is often buried in the album deep cuts that fans love, like "Everything Has Changed" or "Clean." One day, she'll bring us full circle on "Midnight Rain," saying she *is* the title, the embodiment of deep feeling, brave emotional exploration. and even melancholy.

As well as prompting Taylor to expand her songwriting into places we couldn't have imagined, a good thing about the criticism of *Fearless* was that it activated Revenge Taylor, a brilliantly petty Swiftian persona who

13

Taylor has firmly established romantic rain as one of her magic symbols and, from now on, she'll use it sparingly, trusting us to recognize it as a callback to this tender, deeply romantic reference point.

13

would bring us songs like "Look What You Made Me Do" and "Karma." A critic who called Taylor's singing "dreadful" inspired the hall-of-fame retaliation banger "Mean," in which Taylor describes him as a guy getting sloppy-drunk in a sports bar and unable to stop ranting about her. Taylor says she's going to get even by becoming so big and powerful that this critic's words can't hurt her anymore. This came true: no music critic has more power than Taylor Swift these days.

The revenge songs on *Speak Now* were written by a wounded Taylor who lashed out; in 2014 she would say, "An interesting part about having grown up with all of my inner thoughts and lessons and doubts and fears and anger issues being put into these songs and these lyrics is, sometimes, you change your mind."[13] "Better Than Revenge" is one such song. It clearly mirrors the work of Taylor's close friend Hayley Williams, the singer of the emo band Paramore. It is one of Taylor's extremely rare misfires. Paramore's song "Misery Business" shares DNA with "Better Than Revenge": they are both about jealousy and competition between love rivals, which descend into calling the other girl sexualized insults. "Better Than Revenge" is a more straightforward rock song without the bratty tone and hammering guitars of the Paramore song, and with a lyric that mentions the playground, a place Taylor often visits to express bullying, tragically misused here. The most interesting detail is that when she came to rerecord the song as part of *Speak Now (Taylor's Version)*, Taylor expressed regret via a tweak to the lyrics. Ever since the project was announced, fans had debated whether Taylor would, or should, replace the insulting lyric. Taylor moved on from the sentiment long ago: "I was eighteen when I wrote that. That's the age you are when you think someone can actually take your boyfriend. Then you grow up and realize no one can take someone from you if they don't want to leave."[14] Changing the lyric disrupted the project of making the rerecording exactly the same, although it should be noted that Taylor was legally required to make the rerecorded albums distinguishable from the originals.[15] The difference is usually obvious in Taylor's voice, which has become richer with time and training. But perhaps this was a perfect opportunity to make a point of difference and right an old wrong in one fell swoop. In the end, she did change it, singing "matches" in place of "mattress."

Taylor's journey with writing and owning her opinions in the heat of the moment—speak *now*!—adds new meaning to the album's title. Originally intended to be called *Enchanted*, after the swooniest Taylor song of them all, the one about the excitement of meeting someone new, Taylor changed it after input from her label boss, Scott Borchetta. We are not going to like everything Scott does, but he had a sound argument this time. He told her, "Taylor, this record isn't about fairy tales and high school anymore. That's not where you're at."[16] Instead, Taylor named the album after "Speak Now," a track

13

We'll always be able to go back and listen to Taylor's first three albums and dissolve in the fairy lights of it all when we are in the mood.

13

about owning her voice. It's funny and theatrical, but it's not exactly the empowerment anthem you might expect. It does, however, reveal that Taylor is not the wedding-obsessed girl people often assume. Although "Mine" had a proposal-themed video, and Taylor planned yet another onstage wedding for the Speak Now Tour, she explained that she was using it as a symbol, not as a statement of what we should be seeking: "I'm not really that girl who dreams about her wedding day. It just seems like the idealistic, happy-ever-after [moment]. It's funny that my wedding references have all been like 'Marry me, Juliet,' and on my *Speak Now* album I'm ripping one to shreds."[17]

The authentically Swiftian romance on *Speak Now* was harder to let go of: Will there be no more sparkling nights, twirling dresses, and pouring rain? Letting go of girlhood was the hardest of all, both for Taylor and for fans who connected with the iconography of this era. We'll always be able to go back and listen to Taylor's first three albums and dissolve in the fairy lights of it all when we are in the mood. That's what the lavender gown she wears on the Eras Tour to perform "Enchanted" shows us: that Taylor is proud of when she used to sing that "country beep" just for the girls, and she'll never disavow it. The gown itself is a marvel. Made by Nicole + Felicia,[18] it is the sparkliest thing you've ever seen, constructed from five hundred yards of glitter tulle and embellished with three thousand crystals. Its multiple tiers take up acres of space on the stage. It's the girl inside the adult Taylor, kept in a memory box and brought out to twirl under the spotlight she always dreamed of.

Artistically, Taylor had gone as far as she could with the theme of fairy tales and nostalgia for childhood. The next time Taylor would sing about childhood was on her 2021 album, *folklore*, and her perspective would be much changed. Also, Taylor knows better than we do when she needs to reinvent herself. The fans who had grown up alongside her were out in the world now, and they wanted music that helped make sense of their current lives. Although *Speak Now* was a huge commercial success, there wasn't a song that hit as big as "Love Story" or "You Belong With Me." Music is fickle, and Taylor was already "nothing new." In order to stay popular and relevant, she would have to find a way to change. During the *Speak Now* era, Taylor began adjusting everything, from her sound to the team around her. Up until now, her clothes and stage costumes had been bought for her and styled by Sandi Spika Borchetta, Scott's wife and later senior vice president of creative at their label, Big Machine. Around this time, Taylor switched to a new stylist, Joseph Cassell, who remains her fashion stylist to this day. Together, they were about to overhaul her image, armoring her with more intentional looks that helped build her narrative, not just pretty dresses.

Just because the fairy tales are over doesn't mean there are no longer magic symbols to be discovered. A new one had come along in 2009, when Taylor did a photo shoot for the magazine *Allure*. The makeup artist Gucci Westman suggested a particular lip color she thought would look stunning on Taylor. Andrea, Taylor's mom, said no way. Her daughter's image was young, sweet, and not in any way a vamp. But Gucci and Taylor got their way. Taylor had started to let her rage out on her third album, but nowhere does she mention the color that would become her signature. The only hint of what was to come was on the *Speak Now* album cover: her dress is purple, but her lips are burning red.

No Boys Allowed

A PLAYLIST OF TAYLOR SWIFT SONGS NOT ABOUT BOYFRIENDS

FRIENDS AND FANS

- "Long Live"—graduation from school; an anthem for her friends, her bandmates, and, ultimately, for the fandom.
- "When Emma Falls In Love (Taylor's Version) (From The Vault)"—a tender portrait of a friend, assumed to be actor Emma Stone.
- "New Romantics"—partying with your friends is fun.
- "dorothea"—having a friend become famous and you never see them anymore.
- "mirrorball"—Taylor's eternal need to perform for her fans. The bridge touches on the calling-off of the Lover Fest due to Covid-19, and Taylor's adorably effortful personality.

FAMILY

- "The Best Day"—the joy and innocence of childhood.
- "Never Grow Up"—the poignancy of realizing childhood is over; pre-grief at losing your parents.
- "Safe & Sound" (feat. The Civil Wars)—the love of an older sister for the younger one.
- "Ronan"—a memorial to Ronan, the three-year-old son of Maya Thompson (credited as a cowriter), written from her perspective.
- "Soon You'll Get Better"—arguably the most personal song Taylor has ever released and the subject of a Swift family conference to agree whether it should go on the album *Lover*. About Taylor's mother Andrea's cancer diagnosis and treatment, and Taylor's fear of losing her.
- "marjorie"—about the life of Taylor's grandmother Marjorie Finlay, a singer whose voice can be heard in the background singing an aria from the opera *La Rondine* by Puccini.

LIFE

- "A Place In This World"—a very young Taylor wonders what shape her life will take.
- "22"—the struggles and joys of being a young adult, especially Taylor Swift.
- "Welcome To New York"—the excitement of moving to the big city where you can be whoever you want.
- "seven"—memories from Taylor's childhood in Pennsylvania.
- "You're On Your Own, Kid"—a young Taylor realizes that the drive to find love and success is a mixed bag.
- "this is me trying"—the challenges of aimlessness and addiction.
- "evermore (feat. Bon Iver)"—depression.

POLITICS
- "The Man"—FEMINISM.
- "Miss Americana & The Heartbreak Prince"—a haunted high school stands in for the state of America.
- "You Need To Calm Down"—equality! LGBTQ+ rights in particular.
- "Only The Young"—encouraging young people to get involved in politics after the election of Donald Trump.

- "mad woman"—it's feminism again! Although the song is aimed at a couple who have wounded her, it's also about how women's anger makes people uncomfortable.

STORY SONGS

- "the last great american dynasty"—a story based on the life of Rebekah Harkness, whose house in Rhode Island Taylor bought in 2013. If she ever decides to sell, this house should be purchased for the nation and turned into a museum.
- "epiphany"—the experience of war, and of being a health-care worker during the Covid-19 pandemic.
- "no body, no crime (feat. HAIM)"—the story of a retaliatory murder against the man who killed your best friend, and how to get away with it.
- "cowboy like me"—a story song about being a grifter and falling in love anyway.

No Boys Allowed

13

Shout-out Song

"LONG LIVE"

Taylor's teal guitar with decorations of orange koi fish around the center usually lives in the Country Music Hall of Fame. In July 2023, it seemed that a heist had been successfully pulled off, because the guitar had been replaced with a sign stating "artifact temporarily removed." The fifth section of Taylor's show on the Eras Tour is dedicated to *Speak Now*. It ends with "Enchanted," and Taylor walks off in her sparkling gown, ready to return in her "22" incarnation. On July 7, she didn't leave. Instead, she picked up her koi fish guitar and played her song "Long Live," all about her "amazing, incredible, beautiful band of thieves."[19] And the crowd went wild.

It is a testament to Taylor and the excellent relationships she builds that some of her touring band members have been with her since her earliest days onstage, back when she was still the opening act for country veterans like George Strait. Writing a tribute to her band is exactly the kind of personal touch we love her for. The seeds of this anthemic song about loyalty and life on the road were planted in "Change," from *Fearless*, which is about Taylor's hope that she'll make it despite being on a smaller label.[20] She fights battles in both songs, with her small gang of comrades. "Long Live" is more towering and poignant, and more specific in how it captures a blaze of glory, from the confetti that rains down, just like in a live show, to the baseball caps and ripped jeans her band of rugged touring musicians wears.

"Long Live" describes how Taylor and her trusty band smashed through the walls that held her back in the lyrics to "Change." They broke down barriers Taylor faced in music and built her career from the rubble: "This song is about my band, and my producer, and all the people who have helped us build this brick by brick. The fans, the people who I feel that we are all in this together; this song talks about the triumphant moments that we've had in the last two years."[21] That triumph she mentioned was Taylor winning the award for Entertainer of the Year at the Country Music Awards in 2009. The award was presented by Faith Hill and Tim McGraw, who said, "Country music is truly music for everyone. It has never been more apparent with the diversity of tonight's nominees," referring to Taylor, and to one man not wearing a cowboy hat.[22] As part of her speech, Taylor brought her band up onstage to share in the achievement with her, calling out names like Mike Meadows, Amos Heller, and Paul Sidoti, who still play by her side on the Eras Tour. It was a classy move to acknowledge that the live show is built around a band, and no prerecorded backing track could ever replace them.

Fans have adopted "Long Live" as one of their own, seeing themselves reflected in the line about crowds going wild—and making good on it whenever the song is played live. When Taylor accepted her Entertainer of the Year award, she also thanked "the fans who come to the shows with your shirts that you made yourself, and the looks on your face, that's why I do this. Thank you for this moment."[23] As well as being a personal love letter, "Long Live" sounds like a graduation song. The decade was ending; she was memorializing the moment of her greatest successes. After all, she couldn't be sure what would happen next. The song mentions "pretenders," both a reference to insincerity and people who would usurp Taylor's position as the queen. By the time Taylor returned to the CMAs to reclaim her Entertainer of the Year crown in 2011, she had been touring *Speak Now* all year. Country music had changed in this time: only two of the other nominees wore cowboy hats. It just wasn't changing fast enough for Taylor. When she won, she read out a list (written on her arm, just like she wrote lyrics and sayings on her arm for live shows) of the artists she wanted to thank for performing with her on tour. Along with Tim McGraw and Kenny Chesney, she thanked Nicki Minaj and Usher. Clearly, Taylor was making connections outside of country music.

The Taylor who scrawled lyrics and the number 13 on her arm during the Speak Now Tour and sang about dragons and princesses every night was also the Taylor who went through a six-month songwriting drought. She just couldn't find a way to write about what she was going through: "There's a kind of bad that gets so overpowering you can't even write about it. When you feel pain that is so far past dysfunctional, that leaves you with so many emotions that you can't filter them down to simple emotions to write about, that's when you know you really need to get out."[24] Taylor showed up to rehearsal one day "a broken human," thinking she had no songs in her. It was jamming with her band that brought back the creative spark. She sat down and "ended up just playing four chords over and over again. The band started kicking in, like Amos Heller on bass. People just started playing along with me. I think they could tell I was really going through it. And I just started singing, and riffing, and sort of ad-libbing this song that, basically, was"—[25] Can you guess?

I Remember

4

RED

To launch her album *Red* in 2012, Taylor played a handful of new songs to a room of lucky fans, whom she introduced as her "friends." Taylor was mixing things up: the performance was shared over the internet using the relatively new and exciting technology of livestreaming. The music was about to astound people even more than the possibility of watching Taylor talk live on the internet. She strummed her acoustic guitar while sitting in front of a huge banner with her own face on it. In the banner, all you can see are her now-signature red lips and blond hair. On her first three albums, Taylor often wrote about what she could read in someone's eyes, whether they were turned on her from the passenger seat in "Fearless" or whispering to her on "Enchanted." Now, Taylor's muses spoke with lips and hands. With just the tiniest flicker of emotion on her face, Taylor talked about writing the slow, sad fifth track on the album, which she loved but was probably destined to be just a deep cut, rarely spoken about outside the fan forums: "It starts with meeting someone, and all the details about that innocent beginning and it follows the story all the way to the bitter end."[1]

When *Rolling Stone* included *Red* in its 2020 list of the five hundred greatest albums ever made, Taylor described *Red* as a "joyride," a Jackson Pollock–esque "splatter-paint album," and her "only true breakup album."[2] The ninety-ninth greatest album of all time was a chaotic experiment in some ways, which Taylor says is "a metaphor for how messy a real breakup is," with a mix of "Nashville songs" and a new, boppier sound.[3] The big singles on *Red* draw in sounds from across the musical spectrum. What felt to some people like a whiplash amount of genre experimentation in 2012 feels normal now, and Taylor can experiment with almost any sound; in 2023, the BBC described Taylor as a subgenre of music in herself.[4] Seeing Taylor, bedraggled and dirty, in the video for "I Knew You Were Trouble," it's hard to believe this was the same girl who sang "Love Story" and "Mine." The rough genre of the first three albums is teen movie soundtrack–core, while on *Red* Taylor started flexing her pop muscles. Great pop music works hard for our attention and sticks like glue—think of how easily "Shake It Off" gets stuck in your head.

Do you prefer laser-targeted pop hits or poetic, introspective songs? Here's a popstar who can do both. "Red" and "State of Grace" contain a flurry of metaphors and descriptions: he's an unsolvable crossword puzzle and a cannonball crashing into your life. A shout-out to the muses: Taylor finally had some heavyweight personalities in her life who were equal to her ability to write songs about them. The album is still about heartbreak and starlit nights, but Taylor's also trusting us with a more philosophical approach than ever before—something that will only get more impressive in her later albums—writing in the airy opener "State Of Grace" about leaving her relationship in fate's hands. Although everything is changing, Taylor is at pains to make sure her existing fans don't feel too lost: "You want to provide your fans with something exciting, but you don't want them to be listening to the album going 'I don't recognize her.' So somewhere in the middle you have to find a balance. Like a tightrope."[5] More than a decade on, Taylor is still on that tightrope, still trying anything she can to keep us entertained. The songwriter Diane Warren, who cowrote "Say Don't Go (Taylor's Version) (From The Vault)" with Taylor for *1989 (Taylor's Version)*, described how Taylor "gets her audience. She's deeply aware of how her fans want to hear something. I can't explain it, but that's probably why she's the biggest fucking star in the world."[6] No wonder the fan base is dedicated. Has anyone else thought this deeply about what would make fans feel comforted and happy?

Taylor was aware that not everyone thought her music was cool. The guy with his indie records who inspired "We Are Never Ever Getting Back Together" is a stand-in for all the people who have sneered at Taylor or pop music in general: "It was a relationship where I felt very critiqued and subpar. He'd listen to this music that nobody had heard of . . . but as soon as anyone else liked these bands, he'd drop them. I felt that was a strange way to be a music fan. And I couldn't understand why he would never say anything nice about the songs I wrote or the music I made."[7] In hindsight, the musical risks Taylor took on *Red* might seem like a no-brainer, but the history of pop is 99 percent made up of careers that tailed off after the first smash-hit record, let alone the third. We know that Taylor has been able to stay on the tightrope for two decades, but, in 2012, things were delicate. She was painfully aware that you only get a short period of being the ingénue: "At twenty-two I was already watching newer, cooler artists come out every week."[8] The new Taylor called a guy whom she says "taught me more about writing than anyone I can imagine,"[9] who understands pop music in all its sticky and euphoric glory: Max Martin.

The stabbing electric guitars, cascading repetitions, and, most important, the chorus that drops *just* right for supreme drama on "I Knew You Were Trouble" are all Max Martin signatures. If you hear a pop song that is catchy on an elite level, go to Wikipedia and check if Max was behind it. He produced ". . . Baby One More Time" (1998) and "Blinding Lights" (2019), the kind of career longevity and relevance very few people achieve. For this reason, as well as their shared love of dramatically dropping out the music for a massive chorus moment (compare "Love Story" and "I Knew You Were Trouble"), Max and Taylor are a match made in musical heaven. Max has an approach to successful hit-making called "melodic math." This includes rules such as making sure pairs of lines have the same number of syllables, removing distracting clutter from the tune. He also uses "melodic previews," where tiny snippets of the chorus tune will appear in the verse, to create that sense of landing back at home that makes an incredible pop chorus. Taylor previews melodies in a bigger way that creates an even deeper sense of coming home. "I Knew You Were Trouble" may have an intense new dance music sound in it, but it also has what has come to be known as a "T-drop."

Coined by the musicologist Nate Sloan and the songwriter Charlie Harding on the *Switched On Pop* podcast, the T-drop is a sequence of notes that you'll recognize, even if you don't consciously know it yet. Certain melodic signatures connect songs across Taylor's different eras, like the up-and-down zigzags in the melodies of "Forever & Always" and "State Of Grace," both about relationships with major highs and lows. "State Of Grace," *Red*'s scene-setting opener, is stuffed with these kinds of self-quotations. It is built around the T-drop, which is a fourth note that goes to a third note that drops further than you'd expect to a sixth note. Here is a diagram to help explain:

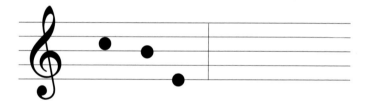

The way Taylor sings "see-ee-ee" and "me-ee-ee" in the chorus of "You Belong With Me" is a clear example. You'll also hear it on "Welcome To New York," grounding us in the Taylor-Verse we know and love even as her sound goes to wild new places. She makes other callbacks too. The fairy tales that were such a key part of *Fearless* and *Speak Now* are here: the opening line of "I Knew You Were Trouble" is "Once upon a time." All along, Taylor has been tying her songs together with these invisible strings.

As well as sprinkling in familiar motifs, Taylor was also breaking new (holy) ground in her songwriting: "I love a bridge so much. I love trying to take the song to a higher level with the bridge."[10] Because you only hear a bridge once, it's a place for the most chaotically emotional statements, from a description of a snowmobile accident ("Out Of The Woods") to a devastating takedown of Taylor's own marriageability ("You're Losing Me"). Taylor's bridges come from a place where verse-chorus structure can't contain her feelings anymore. Although other songwriters also use bridges for contrast, to keep songs exciting, Taylor's bridges are so effective that they often completely transform the song. "Treacherous," from *Red*, is a special example because it's mild and unassuming but, in the bridge, Taylor flips a switch. The subject matter is similar to the bridge of "You Belong With Me": someone drives over to see Taylor in the middle of the night. But "Treacherous" shifts the lyricism up a gear: it's not just late; the night is "sleepless," with headlights alone illuminating the dark. The whole story is boiled down into its key Swiftian details. The structure of "Treacherous" is a new kind of Taylor song, which will eventually be everywhere on the album *folklore*: it begins in a relaxed, contemplative tone and then suddenly breaks out into an emotional bridge that defines the whole song. This structure makes the song feel like Taylor is mulling over a problem and having a sudden breakthrough. Taylor has often described her songs as "like a letter to somebody" ("Dear John" may be the perfect

Because you only hear a
bridge once, it's a place for
the most chaotically emotional
statements, from a description
of a snowmobile accident
("Out Of The Woods") to a
devastating takedown of
Taylor's own marriageability
("You're Losing Me").

example).[11] She is writing her way through a thought and then is suddenly hit with an epiphany and gets excited—or angry.

During the *Red* era, Taylor achieved a new kind of cultural relevance that we're only just starting to look at in the rearview mirror and reassess. Taylor Swift is, as affectionately coined by DJ Louie XIV of the *Pop Pantheon* podcast, the "basic bitch whisperer." Being "basic" was a cultural phenomenon that arose after the death of hipster culture, as sincerity started rising to replace irony as the most important way to be. Taylor's sincerity made her an obvious target for the last gasp of hipsterism, and her music would become an emblematically basic thing to like. In 2014, *TIME* magazine published an article describing Taylor as "Vanilla Coke" and "the sonic version of drinking a pumpkin spice latte in Uggs while watching *Sex and the City*."[12] The article linked to a BuzzFeed quiz that tested "How basic are you?"[13] Among the items that qualified you as basic were "You love Taylor Swift," "You love white wine," "You identify with '22,'" and "You like scented candles" (send us all to basic jail, I guess). The quiz's creator wrote that being basic was "about people who get excited for things that are pretty normal or popular," but it's also a list of things that someone trying to broadcast white femininity would supposedly pretend to like in order to fit in. That's why Taylor doesn't fit on the list alongside Starbucks coffee: no one ever gained clout by liking Taylor, given how passionately unpleasant people have been about her over the years. Taylor was highly aware that she was perceived this way. All popstars are sensitive to what is being said about them, but Taylor was known for being chronically online at this point and still messaging fans even at this level of fame. "22" intentionally creates distance between Taylor and "cool" people who inhabit a "scene," and instead invites in an audience who don't necessarily care about being cool. The lyrics even include a spoken-word line where a Valley-girl type pretends not to know who Taylor Swift is. In the music video, Taylor wears a now-iconic sequined T-shirt reading "Not a lot going on at the moment," an ironic reference to her lack of nonchalance; later, she will use this line as an Instagram caption twice, knowing full well she is about to drop *folklore* and then *evermore*. She doesn't even try to maintain an edgy public persona: "I dance like I'm having fun at awards shows, even though no one else is. Because being cool usually means being bored by everything. And I'm not bored by any of this."[14]

"22" has a sense of humor (that perfectly placed "ew"), an underrated Taylor quality. "I Bet You Think About Me (feat. Chris Stapleton) (Taylor's Version) (From The Vault)" is also funny, with its increasingly deranged list of ways in which the ex is pretentious, and it is stuffed with Taylorisms, like three a.m., a brilliantly delivered disgusted "huh," and the bravado of telling your ex that you know you're still on his mind. It is also a rare song where Taylor touches explicitly on class. It mentions the "pedigree" of the girl this "upper-crust" person replaced her with and the "silver spoon" he was born with. Their differences in class status drive them apart, as well as how relatively "hip" they are (yes, it's that guy again). If we assume it's the same person as described on "All Too Well" and "Begin Again," one of his defining features was that he wouldn't laugh at Taylor's jokes. This is especially sad because her partner's laugh is a key element of Taylor's ideal love, present from "Our Song" through "Jump Then Fall," "Ours," and especially "New Year's Day," where she fears losing her person and his laugh. The inclusion of "Starlight" over so many excellent vault songs may have been about correcting the class snobbery that stung Taylor. It's the love story of Ethel and Robert Kennedy, members of the Kennedy family often called "American royalty." It shares the word *marvelous* with "the last great american dynasty," which suggests Taylor associates the word with dynasties. If you wonder where Taylor gets so many ideas, she wrote "Starlight" by looking through old photographs and imagining how Ethel and Robert met, just like she does in the antiques shop in "Timeless (Taylor's Version) (From The Vault)," from *Speak Now (Taylor's Version)*.

Taylor is not longing for a night from the past; it's tonight.

In a very Taylor move, she later became friends with Ethel and briefly owned the house next to hers in Hyannis Port, before eventually buying Holiday House, the setting for "the last great american dynasty."[15]

Although "Starlight" and songs like "All Too Well," the ruby in *Red*'s crown, are all about memory, this album is also dragging itself into the present. "22" is one of Taylor's first songs since the track "Fearless" to feel like it's completely rooted in the present moment. That's a major feature of pop, after all: the aim is to be right here, right now. In "22," Taylor is not longing for a night from the past; it's tonight. It's also an important corrective to the songs that zoom in extremely close on her partner. After all, part of a breakup is dusting yourself off and going out with your friends. Tiring of the endless narrative around her dating life, Taylor was already building friendship into her image. Still besties with Abigail from "Fifteen," she also shouted out four of her friends in the *Red* liner notes, in a secret message hidden in the lyrics for "22." The duet "Everything Has Changed" with Ed Sheeran is one of two successful duets with men on the album, and Taylor has described him as "one of my best friends, who took me to pubs and taught me how to make a good cup of tea."[16]

Those hidden messages were so fun. When *Red* came out, the dazzling lyrics made you want to lie on the floor and read the CD booklet, and of course study the pictures of Taylor looking chic in her high-waisted shorts and felt hat. Either you spotted the capitalized letters in the lyrics yourself, like some kind of mastermind, or another fan tipped you off that there was something to look for, as there had been in previous booklets. Armed with pen and paper, you had to meticulously copy each letter until a word or phrase emerged. Taylor never lets Swifties rest, even to this day: in the run-up to releasing *1989 (Taylor's Version)*, fans had to collectively crack 33 million mini puzzles to find out the track names.[17] It's hard to exaggerate how much of a strategist Taylor is. At a listening party for *Red* in 2012, she spoke about her songwriting, as she always gently but firmly does when speaking about her career: "The thing about a song is that it's a little message in a bottle."[18] Presumably, she was giggling very hard in the privacy of her own head, knowing that "Message In A Bottle (Taylor's Version) (From The Vault)" was lying in her vault, where it would remain a secret for the next nine years.

The hidden message for "Begin Again," the final track on *Red*, is possibly the most poignant one. It reads "I wear heels now." It's a little clue that we're on the journey beyond a focus on romantic love as the be-all and end-all, and in favor of Taylor building her own identity, doing and wearing what she wants, unapologetically. She does not need to make herself smaller to smooth over someone

It's a little clue that we're on the journey beyond a focus on romantic love as the be-all and end-all, and in favor of Taylor building her own identity, doing and wearing what she wants, unapologetically.

else's insecurities. After all, the hidden message for "We Are Never Ever Getting Back Together" is "When I stopped caring what you thought." She might, finally, be over the tragic romance that had her searching in vain for her old self. As she hypes herself up for a first date with someone new, she looks in the mirror and puts in headphones to listen to her own choice of music. If it's *Red*, it's the sound of hope and new beginnings. If it's *Red*, the final song is also an instruction to the stunned person who just listened to a record that changed their life and is ready to listen for the second, third, and hundredth time: begin again.

RED

Shout-out Song

"ALL TOO WELL"

The word *iconic* has become overused, but the fifth song on *Red* has developed iconic status among songs about lost love. It has everything Taylor has come to represent: personal revelations, detailed storytelling, and the raking over of bittersweet memories. The original five-and-a-half-minute version described the way heartbreak can leave you crushed and feeling like a stranger in your own life. The ten-minute version is an epic description of a relationship that left Taylor devastated, starting with one tiny detail and spiraling through the humiliations and betrayals until she's left in a frozen landscape with nothing to cling to but the right to remember.

Taylor says the fifth track on each of her albums is always "really honest, emotional, vulnerable, and personal."[19] "All Too Well" is the crowning glory of all Track Fives. After writing the majority of it by ad-libbing during a jam with her band, Taylor realized that she had too much song on her hands, and called the songwriter Liz Rose, with whom she had cowritten fourteen previous songs. "It clocked in at around ten minutes," Taylor says. "We set out editing, trimming, cutting out big sections until it was a reasonable five minutes and thirty seconds."[20] When

Red was released, fans started to talk about this song that spoke to them so deeply. Taylor herself was surprised that it became such a favorite. She had feared it was too raw, and perhaps it's also surprising that a song so specific to her own experience could touch a chord in so many people. Like many of her songs, it is an open letter to the person who hurt her. But the specifics, like the falling autumn leaves and cold air of their trip to upstate New York, where Taylor is sure they'll finally exchange "I love yous" make it feel so real. One image in particular has become very meaningful: the scarf, which Taylor calls "a metaphor" for the part of her that she left behind in the relationship.[21] Then there's the image of dancing around in the kitchen, which so many people hold up as a romantic ideal. But the line that people scream and roar is from the bridge, where the person Taylor once loved reaches out, not to reignite what they once had, but to break her heart again, crumpling it up and throwing it away as if it was nothing.

Nine years later, rumors of an extended recording of the song turned out to be true. "All Too Well (10 Minute Version) (Taylor's Version) (From The Vault)" was included as the final track on *Red (Taylor's Version)*. Taylor revealed a song that was even more withering about the foibles of this man who toyed with her emotions until he finally let them thud to the ground, like the car keys he carelessly tosses at her in the accompanying short film. The sad but tender lyrics of the original version, where his mother showed Taylor pictures of him as a child, give way to a portrait of a pretentious person more interested in being charming than sincere. His inauthentic love has drained Taylor, leaving her a skeletal wreck who no longer feels tenderness, or excitement, but only shame. It became an unusual Billboard Hot 100 number one in November 2021. As well as being a total downer in the best way, "All Too Well" (10 Minute Version) (Taylor's Version) (From The Vault)" is, obviously, ten minutes long. It broke the record for longest number one song in the US, held for fifty years by Don McLean for "American Pie" (Taylor sent him flowers to commiserate).

Before the song came out, some assumed that it would be four and a half extra minutes of what we already had. That would have been nice, but hardly revelatory, and maybe even have risked outstaying its welcome. Instead, new melodies are introduced to vary the song's constant climb to an apparent crescendo. The new outro comes as a revelation. The music has been building under each detailed, tortured line, but instead of reaching a moment of triumph or catharsis, it suddenly drops out and becomes sparse and slow. The sparse music reflects the story of their love: all that expectation, and it only left her with emptiness. As the music fades away, Taylor asks the kind of question you put to someone who is leaving you: Is this hurting you too? The lush colors of autumn are gone, Taylor is back in the city, and snow is falling. The one saving grace is that she wrote it all down. No one can ever take her version of events from her: she was there, and she remembers.

Taylor performed the ten-minute version of "All Too Well" for the first time in a spine-tingling live rendition on *Saturday Night Live*. With the short film playing in the background, we saw actor Sadie Sink portray a younger Taylor, happy and in love, then sobbing in agony, and eventually writing the story of what happened to her. The video ends with Taylor as an author in a bookstore, reading her story to a rapt audience. When she first played "All Too Well" on tour, she used to look so sad. Over time, playing the song and hearing fans singing their hearts out to it, adopting it as their own, has changed how she sees it: "For me, this song has turned into a story of what the fans did."[22] It is the Swiftie international anthem.

New York

Streets

and Electric

Beats

1989

1989 is as meticulously mapped out as the New York streets (and a lot cleaner). Like all major urban areas, it offers a fresh start to anyone who needs it. Taylor explains it in the scene-setting opener, "Welcome To New York"—the city is a place where you are liberated to be whoever you want and desire whomever you want. In this urban forest, she has a chance to escape the media scrutiny she describes on "Blank Space," "Shake It Off," and "I Know Places." Taylor has found her new sound: crisp drum-machines; eighties-style synth; and heavier, distorted bass, like you'd hear coming from the neighborhood dive bar at two in the morning. Taylor is a delighted tourist, simply thrilled with everything about New York. She would even become a "welcome ambassador"; cynical New Yorkers were a little jaded at hearing "Welcome To New York" in every cab they took for a year after the release of *1989*. But Taylor never became jaded: "It's like an electric city, and I approached moving there with such wide-eyed optimism."[1] The city that never sleeps is perfect for this insomniac: midnight is a normal time to be awake in NYC. Songs about running around town, like "Wonderland" and "New Romantics," portray New York as Taylor's magical adventure playground, a surreal *Alice in Wonderland* landscape caught in Polaroid snapshots rather than artfully posed photos. She can be anyone there, so she decides to be the greatest pop musician of the twenty-first century.

Taylor calls *1989* her "first documented, official pop album."[2] From "Baby Love" by The Supremes to "Blank

Space," "perfect pop" has a robust musical structure that holds you, a universal message, and something a little spicy to keep you coming back. It's like falling in love, bottled into three and a half minutes. Pop should also not waste one second of your precious time—you're a busy person about town! This album is pared back to only what you need: *Red* opened with a song that was nearly five minutes long, but on *1989* Taylor only lets herself go over four minutes later in the album, on Nashville callbacks like "How You Get The Girl." At that point, she's confident that she has hooked you in with the greatest single run of pop songs ever. There is no mightier, more jaw-droppingly entertaining sequence than "Blank Space," "Style," "Out Of The Woods," "All You Had To Do Was Stay," "Shake It Off," and "I Wish You Would."

By *1989* Taylor has already experienced the beginning and end of relationships, and she's started to notice the pattern. *1989*, named for the year of Taylor's birth and with a retro sound, is about endlessly returning to memories in an apparently inescapable cycle. Naming the album after the

She can be anyone there, so she decides to be the greatest pop musician of the twenty-first century.

Naming the album after the year of her birth is almost like naming it after herself, if she hadn't already released *Taylor Swift*. However, the story of this album is mostly about the destabilizing effect of a cat-and-mouse relationship that never quite made it to love, examining in detail the confusing zone between nothing and something real.

year of her birth is almost like naming it after herself, if she hadn't already released *Taylor Swift*. However, the story of this album is mostly about the destabilizing effect of a cat-and-mouse relationship that never quite made it to love, examining in detail the confusing zone between nothing and something real. On "Style," the lovers circle each other endlessly, not in a romantic snow globe like in the gorgeous bonus track "You Are In Love," but as if they're trapped in an exhausting situationship that never leads anywhere. Taylor remains trapped in her cycle until "Clean." In what became known as the "Clean Speech," Taylor introduced the song during the 1989 Tour, talking about the resilience it takes to continue going forward even after making mistakes:

> *[I]n twenty-five years I've learned that making mistakes and feeling pain is terrible, but it makes you stronger. And going through terrible things and continuing to move forward doesn't make you damaged goods, it makes you clean.*[3]

She escaped this particular man, but cycles will come back again and again in her music, reflecting how long it takes to process memories: on "right where you left me" (*evermore*), Taylor watches life fly past her while she remains stuck in the restaurant, unable to get off the treadmill of her thoughts.

On *1989*, Taylor also examines her fraught relationship with her own celebrity and how the media chooses to speak about her. While on "22" she sang to someone who didn't know about her, on "Blank Space" she says she knows full well her new love interest must have heard about her (she is Taylor Swift, after all). Like many young women, Taylor has to tussle with the fact that she wants to be seen and attract attention, but some people take that as a license to leer and comment on her appearance and her behavior, both of which have nothing to do with them. Taylor had teased names and told stories about some of her relationships in her previous music, and this quickly became the only hook publications used to write stories about her—something she in turn used to create a satirical version of herself as presented by the media:

> [T]hat's actually a really kind of interesting character they're writing about. She jet-sets around the world, collecting men, and she can get any of them . . . but she's so clingy, so they leave and she cries and then she gets another one in her web and she traps them and locks them in her mansion.[4]

Taylor needed a new narrative for the media to grab on to. Her musical response to the media interest in her love life was "Blank Space," which could be read as a straightforward song about *1989*'s on-off relationship but is much sharper and funnier when you understand that Taylor is playing the character of a female Bluebeard who constantly needs fresh cute-boy blood. It's a wither-ing put-down, with a music video where Taylor portrays a deranged woman who hits a sports car with a golf club and stands on a horse. Only Taylor could write a satire and send it to number one on the Billboard chart.

Another never-ending nightmare Taylor couldn't escape from was an assumption that she didn't write her own songs: she would often hear, "There's no way that she actually carried her weight in those writing sessions."[5] Taylor is fierce in fighting this assumption: "I'm not going to be one of those artists who walks in and says, 'I don't know, what do you want to write about?' or one of those things where they say, 'So what's going on in your life?' and I tell them and then they have to write a song about it. I wouldn't be a singer if I weren't a songwriter. I have no interest in singing some-one else's words."[6] As part of her effort to correct this idea, *1989* came with recordings of the songwriting process, an opportunity to listen to the very moment an idea becomes a song. In one, Taylor plays her first sketch of "Blank Space" to Max Martin and his collaborator Johan Shellback. She has the basic tune, the concept, and hardly any words—this is not her diaristic singer-songwriter mode, where songs are written word by word like a poem. Instead, Taylor has put up the steel structure of a skyscraper and now they have to add the walls and windows. Max and Johan immediately start throwing in the tiny pieces of punctuation that make their songs so catchy: an "oh" here, a different "oh" there, each making the main tune more satisfying.

The Swedes give Taylor plenty of positive reinforcement, and when she throws in the cheeky clicking noise that will become the pen-click, Max shouts, "That's awesome, I love [that], it's so annoying! Everyone's going to kill you."[7] Taylor will work with Max and Johan again on *reputation*, and a video diary will give another window into the fluidity of their collaboration and how pop cowriting works. Sitting on a sofa in Max's studio, Taylor sings the verse of "King Of My Heart" and Johan instantly improvises the pre-chorus. Seconds later, Taylor is singing along to the new melody, some words about being the American dream. Max, with his long hair pulled into an elegant low bun, fills in the keyboard sounds using one of a huge array of carefully tuned instruments. Although some of Taylor's songs are written in twenty minutes flat, like "Love Story," this shows the hard work that goes into crafting an album.

For their super-glue masterpiece "Shake It Off," Taylor and the Swedes recorded their feet hitting the floor, subliminally creating a call to action. Taylor had never previously made proper dancing music, although she started practicing while writing songs for *Red*—the track "Message In A Bottle (Taylor's Version) (From The Vault)" is a great dance-floor starter for a party. Taylor set out to create a truly democratic dance song that required no skill or even enthusiasm to dance to: "I want it to be the song where, like, if it's played at a wedding, and there's this one girl who hasn't danced all night at the reception, all her friends come over to her and they're like, 'You have to dance! Come on! You have to dance on this one!'"[8] There's a video of a twenty-five-year-old Taylor and forty-three-year-old Max Martin singing backing vocals, dancing with equal gusto and pulling silly faces in the vocal booth. It's a hint of how the song makes your dancing muscles twitch, no matter who you are. Taylor played an open-air festival in the UK in 2015, to a crowd who wanted a good day out, for free, and had mostly never heard of this "Tyler Swiff" girl. They probably hadn't seen the perky video where ordinary-looking people dance to "Shake It Off." When Taylor started to play, a lot of the crowd was sitting in deck chairs. By the end of the song, the field was a jubilant mass of kids, dads, teenagers, aunties, and every other stripe of person jigging and jiving for their lives.

"Shake It Off" is the bubblegum high point of *1989*, containing the album's only Taylor laugh (being a popstar is a serious business). Across much of the album, angry or melancholy subject matter is presented within a polished pop sound. When Taylor sings about dancing on her own, she's referencing the work of Swedish singer Robyn, the originator of the subgenre "crying in the club." Robyn's songs "Dancing On My Own" and "Call Your Girlfriend" defied the convention that a pop sound meant the content of the song must be lighthearted and upbeat. Instead, she used the pulsing sounds of synths and the euphoria of an explosive chorus to intensify sadness. The influence of Robyn's "With Every Heartbeat" can be heard on Taylor's "Wildest Dreams"; both use a dreamy synth and a heartbeat-like rhythm. Taylor's song uses a recording of her own heart, bringing us as close as possible to her through sound. "With Every Heartbeat" never resolves into a chorus, which leaves the listener feeling anxious, ready to play it again in case this time the outcome is different. Although Taylor always gives a chorus, the theme of anxiety runs throughout *1989*, as Taylor cycles endlessly around an obsession with the bad boy, the only one who can ease the anxiety he created. Taylor's fears about the relationship are exacerbated by being in the public eye. She told *Rolling Stone* in 2014 that she doesn't appreciate the jokes about her love life because they diminish her work and result in a "pressure so high in a new relationship that it gets snuffed out before it even has a chance to start."[9]

This is Taylor, an "enthusiastic optimist,"[10] so she keeps it positive, playing some very entertaining games with her

"Wildest Dreams" uses a recording of
her own heart, bringing us as close
as possible to her through sound.

media presence. Since *Fearless*, her muses have been creative people, including fellow musicians, with the means and opportunity to create their own art and narrative in response to hers. Celebrity couples often find that being in the same place at the same time ("conflicting schedules") becomes a challenge. On *1989*, Taylor finds an exciting, mysterious muse who can never quite be pinned down. She uses cinematic descriptions to immortalize this person as one of music's greatest heartthrobs: an enigmatic, glamorous figure who drives fast cars under cover of darkness. She compares him to the legendary James Dean, the ultimate bad boy in a leather jacket. The song "Slut! (Taylor's Version) (From The Vault)" gives this portrait more colors by also calling him a "gentleman." It's a flattering portrayal. The visuals add another dimension: the music video for "Style" shows a man holding up a broken mirror that covers his own mouth with Taylor's red lips, combining his hunky masculinity with Taylor's super-femininity. When he glances in the (very Swiftian) rearview mirror, he sees her looking back at him. He's her male mirror image.

While promoting the album, Taylor insisted that she had never named the inspiration for "Style." This message was intended for pop radio listeners. The paper-airplane necklace she wore in the video and referenced in the lyrics to "Out Of The Woods" told its own story for people who had traced the necklace's ownership and knew it was a love token that symbolized a particular relationship. It just shows that Taylor was already mirrorballing: showing a different facet of herself to different listeners, depending on who you are and what you need. Taylor works hard at this, telling *Wonderland* in 2014: "I think people want art to have layers. I think that they want to know that there's a meaning and a story . . . they want to know that there are secrets that they have the option of figuring out."[11] Celebrity scandals, like the alleged inter-popstar beef around "Bad Blood," helped to sell the album using headlines as free marketing, but the music always stands on its own two feet. It's also fine to ignore the celebrity aspect and keep these stories private and precious—just you and the song, dancing in your snow globe. Taylor said, "There's a reason there are not any overt callouts in that song. My intent was not to create some gossip-fest. I wanted people to apply it to a situation where they felt betrayed in their own lives."[12] In the liner notes, she wrote just for the fans that the songs had been about her life, but now they were about theirs.

On *1989*, Taylor guaranteed her place in pop music history. It's not just about scoring number ones; it's about recording songs that become red-lip, classic songs that we *love*. Taylor's pop genius lies in how brilliantly she entertains us, combined with how she weaves in themes that touch us personally. She was the ultimate controlling hand on this project, even more than on *Speak Now*, where she wrote every song alone. In an in-depth interview she gave to the Recording Academy about the writing of *1989*, she seemed restless about record label executives' opinions on her music, saying, "[Scott Borchetta] went into a state of semi-panic and went through all the stages of grief—the pleading, the denial. 'Can you give me three country songs? Can we put a fiddle on "Shake It Off"?' And all my answers were a very firm 'no.'"[13] Taylor stood by her creative choices, and they paid off. *1989* sold a million copies in a week. The following year, Taylor made her stand for all musicians when she removed her music from streaming services until a better financial agreement could be reached. She was confident, in control, and on a career high: "This year has been my favorite year of my life so far. I got to make an album exactly the way I wanted to make it. I got to put it out exactly the way that I dreamed of putting it out."[14]

What could possibly go wrong?

Shout-out Song
"OUT OF THE WOODS"

OOOOOOOOOOH OOOOOOOOOOH!

In "Out Of The Woods," Taylor weaves her voice around a strange, shambolic backing track supplied by friend and production partner Jack Antonoff. The song is about how Taylor felt in her cat-and-mouse *1989* love story: "the number one feeling I felt in the whole relationship was anxiety."[15] That sense of overwhelm is built into the music itself: The snare-drum sound is made from white noise and the sound of Jack dropping a bag of equipment. The truncated clips of his voice that open the track are repeated over and over, snipped off abruptly like the relationship itself. It's chaotic and destabilizing. This gives it a sense of danger that reflects Taylor's begging question, which she repeats relentlessly throughout the chorus. Are she and her muse "out of the woods"? All put together, it's the sound of uncertainty.

This song will not let us feel safe for a second, but it will make it beautiful. Taylor said that her perspective on love had changed completely when she wrote *1989*: "I used to think that, you know, you find 'the one.' And it's happily ever after, and it's never a struggle after that. You have a few experiences with love and relationships, and you learn that that's not the case at all. Lots of things are gray areas and complicated situations."[16] "Out Of The Woods" captures the feeling of teetering on the edge of love but never getting there. Strangely, after enough relistens (about a hundred should do it) the song's repetitions become a soothing mantra. And on your worst days, that's when you need a pep talk from the most fist-pumping Swiftian bridge of them all.

The love in "Out Of The Woods" has the potential to be Taylor's domestic dream, with dancing around the living room and lying on the couch together. They take Polaroid portraits, capturing moments that are ultimately all Taylor gets to keep. A sense of coming home is created by a secret T-drop in an ad-libbed "oh" during the second chorus. Has any song ever done more with "oh"? But it's not to be. The lovers are paper airplanes shooting off in different directions. The crashing, maximalist bridge (choral singing; the sound of water dripping; every drum on earth playing at the same time) races through events: an accident, a hospital, both of them crying. Taylor leaves. Taylor comes back. After this perilous night, he's looking at her, which he always does—even when he's driving, he's looking at her with his green eyes. But in the end, it's uncertain what this actually means.

Can Taylor escape the cycles that haunt her throughout *1989*? Not in "Out Of The Woods," as its lack of closure makes it a soundtrack for impossible, irresolvable situations. It also has a poignant echo of "All Too Well," as Taylor tells us that she remembers. On *Midnights*, Taylor will revisit this shaky ground by sampling the "Out Of The Woods" line about remembering on "Question . . . ?" In this song, she adds yet more detailed questions to her list. Will they ever be "out of the woods"? She clearly never got her answer.

6

Snakes and Ladders

REPUTATION

*T*he 1989 Tour ran from May to December 2015, and after all those months of organizing special secret surprise guests and performing for hours most nights, Taylor decided she deserved some time off. Talking with *Vogue* in 2016, Taylor acknowledged the incredible year she had in 2015, but said she was looking forward to taking a break for the first time in a decade.[1]

Taylor did take a break, although it didn't go quite as expected. Usually she released albums on a reliable two-year schedule. But 2016 came and went. Then finally, in 2017, a sign appeared. The images Taylor used to create a narrative around her albums were usually soft and light: butterflies, heart-shaped sunglasses, retro swimsuits, and flamingo pool floats. The saddest, most emotionally loaded symbol in her history to date was probably the scarf. So nothing prepared Swifties for August 21, 2017, when Taylor posted glitchy videos of a hissing snake, ready to attack, across her social media. Two days later, she released the cover of her new album. Her hair looked wet, her lips painted dark red. Was this really Taylor Swift?

Speculation raged about the genre of the new album in the run-up to the release. The ragged torn top she wore on the cover hinted at grunge rock—Taylor had started doing a rock version of "We Are Never Ever Getting Back Together" on tour. The Gothic font looked like a 1990s hip-hop record such as Nas's *Illmatic*, introducing the possibility that Taylor was going full hip-hop. The font was also close to that of the *New York Times* and other newspapers around the world, and newsprint was superimposed over her face. This hinted at 2017's media talking point, "fake news," as well as referencing Britney Spears's video for "Piece Of Me" (2007), a media diss track that also rhymed "karma" with "drama," and had heavily synthesized, pitch-shifted vocals. Taylor had never had visuals this layered before. It was only one image, but it was the first indication of what had

been going on with her since she had vanished from the limelight in 2016.

The first single, "Look What You Made Me Do," was a reset for Taylor musically and in terms of her whole brand as a popstar. It was also a treasure hunt to find all the other music it was referencing. The creepy funhouse-music opening let us know that this song would be dark. The bass is distorted to the point of fuzz. The chorus to "Look What You Made Me Do" is what's known as an anti-chorus: instead of turning full and loud, it's minimalist and subdued; the producer Jack Antonoff described it as "German-sounding," probably meaning the bass-heavy house and techno sound popular in Berlin. This is just the start of the dance music references on reputation, almost as revelatory as the dubstep drop on Red's "I Knew You Were Trouble." "Look What You Made Me Do" also has a theatrical pre-chorus with an incredible twelve repeated identical notes. Relentless staccato notes like this are the unofficial sound of female rage in songs ranging from Mozart's "Queen Of The Night" aria (opening words "The vengeance of Hell boils in my heart") to Kelis's "Caught Out There." Taylor delivers her vocals in a cool and controlled way that is even more unsettling than if she was yelling, although deep in the background vocals you can hear a scream.

When the video dropped a few days later, the suspicions raised by the song were confirmed: this was a whole new Taylor that combined pop-girl presentation with angry, vengeful themes. The "Look What You Made Me Do" music video is a Renaissance painting's worth of symbols and references. Panning over a haunted house on a hill and a graveyard, the camera zooms to a grave that says, "Here Lies Taylor Swift's Reputation." A second later, a zombie Taylor bursts out of the grave. Taylor had never previously looked anything but glamorous, even when she fell in mud in the video for "Out Of The Woods." Zombie Taylor is wearing the same blue dress from "Out Of The Woods," but she doesn't just have a mud-stained dress—she's decomposing entirely. We see Taylor soaking up the attention of the paparazzi even after a car crash, with her pet leopard sitting beside her, a very different cat to her usual fluffy companions. She's also the head of an army of model-like robots, and the Queen of Snakes, sitting on a throne surrounded by slithering reptiles. Although there had previously been the secret messages in liner notes, *reputation* was when hunting for Easter eggs became a major pastime for fans. In the graveyard you can see a stone engraved with "Nils Sjöberg," the pseudonym Taylor used to write the Rihanna song "This Is What You Came For." An enduring mystery was created by the section where Taylor, dressed in prison-issue orange, swings back and forth inside a golden cage. In the poems that accompanied the deluxe editions, she described a "justice system" in her own head that she used to judge her enemies, who themselves become the bars of a "golden prison." In "So It Goes . . ." she also mentions being a hostage in a golden cage. Many moons later, Taylor would appear as a golden Lady Justice in the video for "Karma," echoing the lyrics about karma being a form of justice, albeit one beyond Taylor's control. She's cool with that these days: "There's no point in actively trying to quote unquote defeat your enemies. Trash takes itself out every single time."[2]

In "Look What You Made Me Do," Taylor dances in a way we had not seen before: full popstar choreography. There's dancing in the lyrics across her catalog, but it's romantic dancing around the kitchen or twirling in a dress. Live on tour, her signature dance move was strutting and pointing. In the video for "Shake It Off," she made a point of showing that she didn't have the skills for ballet, breakdancing, twerking, or cheerleading. But now she was seemingly taking inspiration from Lady Gaga, leading a choreographed dance with an all-male troupe in black crop tops and glitter eye makeup. Dance has become an especially important way for Taylor to express rage. On the Eras Tour, she does a *Chicago*-esque slinky chair dance to the seething "Vigilante Shit" (*Midnights*) that brings back memories of "Look What You Made Me Do."

In the second half of *reputation*, Taylor seems to move on (a little) and be able to laugh at what happened. "This Is Why We Can't Have Nice Things" is clearly still about the same betrayal but it is funny and whimsical, both savage and fun, with lyrics about champagne and parties. A reference to F. Scott Fitzgerald's *The Great Gatsby* makes it clear the party is doomed to end tragically, but the song is still a bop. "Gorgeous" describes meeting someone new and gives a shout-out to Taylor's cats, Olivia and Meredith. Along with her mother, Andrea, Taylor's cats were a source of comfort during her tough time, and the deluxe version of the album came with multiple pictures of them. However, cats are also a symbol of revenge for Taylor. When she and her crew are robbing the vault of a streaming company in the "Look What You Made Me Do" video, they wear cat masks. "Vigilante Shit" references cat-eye makeup, while "Karma" compares justice to a cat: a cold-blooded killer to everyone except Taylor, whom it loves.

Another kind of crime is committed in "Getaway Car." A satisfying combination of Nashville-style songwriting and Bon Jovi–style yell-able lines, it tells the story of two Bonnie and Clyde–esque robbers and the heist they pulled on Bonnie's ex. In the end, Bonnie abandons the new guy who helped her escape from the old one, saying he really should've known better. The lyrics refer to where they "met," inviting memories of Taylor's appearance at the 2016 Met Gala. She had the lightened platinum-blond hair referenced in "Dress," another song that mentions where Taylor "met" someone (the Met Gala 2016 after-party must have been incredible). Taylor's documentary *Miss Americana* shows the exact moment the song's bridge was written. Jack Antonoff plays the backing track and tries to rhyme "getaway car" with "I'm losing my . . . something." Taylor suggests "motel bar" and the words fly back and forth between them as the whole bridge unfurls in a matter of seconds. "Argh!" Taylor shouts ecstatically. Jack has said, "That is the only time in my life, in the millions of hours I've spent in studios, that a camera was ever on when magic actually happened."[3]

 Insights to the songwriting process for *reputation* are like gold dust. To preserve her calm and quiet life, and to emphasize the vanishing act she'd pulled earlier in 2017 ("no one physically saw me for a year"),[4] Taylor chose not to do press interviews. Instead of her usual songwriting insights and appearances on talk shows to discuss music, life, and touring, she posted a picture on Instagram captioned:

> *There will be no further explanation.*
> *There will just be reputation.*

Interpretation of the album came entirely through the music and the puzzle pieces fans were able to piece together from the Secret Sessions. Yes, in the midst of her retreat from the world, Taylor still invited hand-picked fans to her home to hear the new album. She hugged people, danced, and made them feel like they'd just met a friend. Her silence also made it possible for us to find our own meaning in the songs, and the era as a whole. "In my rep era" is a useful phrase that has come to mean a time in your life that includes chaos and destruction but is ultimately a relief from people-pleasing.

"Look What You Made Me Do" was a huge number one hit. Taylor had been "extremely focused and specific on a vibe,"[5] according to Jack. Her instincts for where culture was heading were accurate. The Billboard number one in the US after Taylor's song was Cardi B's first hit, "Bodak Yellow." The song has a creepy synth line under it similar to the one from "Look What You Made Me Do," and in the video Cardi has a pet cheetah and spills a bag of diamonds. Clearly, there was something in the water in 2017. But although the videos for "Look What You Made Me Do" and the tropical ". . . Ready For It?" aimed to present Taylor as a tough woman of the streets, both had undercurrents of her signature playfulness. The sexy vacation romance imagery of ". . . Ready for It?" and its clever lyrics, which used tricks like picking up on the last sound of the word "island" and repeating it to start the next sentence, like some kind of intricate puzzle, sounded fun, not dark and angry. When fans heard the whole album, with many love songs such as "Delicate," it was clear there was more to *reputation* than its dark side.

If *reputation* is a slithery snake with a tender and wholesome underbelly, the opposite is usually true in pop music. Taylor's image had been carefully protected to avoid the kind of nasty media treatment other female celebrities received, especially ones who started their career as teenagers, like Britney Spears. Taylor grew up watching the celebrity teenagers of the generation before her publicly explode. Paparazzi photos of Britney in severe mental distress were the most widely circulated images of 2007. Taylor had described how "every other person would say to us, 'Are you going to become a train-wreck? When are we going to see you going off the rails like . . . ,' and then they would name these other girls that they perceived to be trainwrecks."[6] By dressing conservatively and being cautious not to even "be seen holding a glass that they could think alcohol is in,"[7] Taylor had managed to avoid the nastier kinds of media coverage and had mostly experienced just sniping about her love life and how manufactured her image was. In 2016, her castle came crumbling down.

A year before she posted the hissing snakes to her social media, Taylor wrote in her diary on August 29, 2016, "this summer is the apocalypse."[8] The crashed car surrounded by paparazzi in "Look What You Made Me Do" represents her trainwreck: "getting canceled within an inch of my life and sanity," as public opinion appeared to turn on her, resulting in vast numbers of snake emojis being posted in her comments during the infamous "Taylor Swift

Is Over Party."[9] Although Taylor's clap-back project, *reputation*, sold well, it could have gone so differently. Music megastars from Mariah Carey to The Chicks have had their careers dented and derailed for everything from starring in a flop movie to stating their political opinions. We don't know what was said behind the scenes at the record company, but Taylor is clear: "Make no mistake— my career was taken away from me [. . .] That took me down psychologically to a place I've never been before. I moved to a foreign country. I didn't leave a rental house for a year [. . .] I went down really, really hard."[10] It's not hard to connect to this feeling, for anyone who has ever felt like a failure, or been betrayed by people they trusted. It's devastating. In the blink of an eye, Taylor went from being a beloved entertainer and "good girl" to (supposedly) a snake and a villain.

Taylor has often struggled with the good girl/bad girl binary: "My entire moral code, as a kid and now, is a need to be thought of as good. It was all I wrote about. It was all I wanted."[11] She described herself as a good girl in "Sad Beautiful Tragic" and "Style," and although she'd been toying with bad-girl aesthetics, it never went further than getting the girl gang together to stomp around in catsuits in "Bad Blood," or having a visible bra in the video for "I Don't Wanna Live Forever," a song for the *Fifty Shades Darker* soundtrack. Being made to feel like a bad person cut deep for Taylor: in *Miss Americana* she said that popstars are "people who got into this line of work because we wanted people to like us, because we were intrinsically insecure, because we liked the sound of people clapping because it made us forget about how much we feel like we're not good enough."[12] On "I Did Something Bad," Taylor tested what it would be like not to live under this kind of pressure. For once, it's her giving men the runaround, and she says it's fun! It's exciting to hear a chaotic, immoral Taylor on record, something that was a massive change from the Taylor fans had been used to until this album. In the end, though, pretending not to care just wasn't Taylor. She went down fighting—there are references to weapons across *reputation*: guns, knives, pitchforks, poison, and even an axe on the vicious but bouncy "This Is Why We Can't Have Nice Things." But she did go down: not even Taylor would try to claim she triumphed in this war of words, as, in "Call It What You Want," she talks about bringing "a knife to a gun fight" to express just how ill prepared she was to handle what happened in 2016. Instead of burying her

Instead of burying her foes, *reputation* has become a touchstone for vulnerability, which is why it is one of her most important albums.

foes, *reputation* has become a touchstone for vulnerability, which is why it is one of her most important albums. It acknowledges how messy the worst of times are: when they happen in real life, it's impossible to be the equivalent of "Shake It Off" Taylor. However, *reputation* also reminds listeners that horrible situations can lead to new beginnings.

Taylor now says that *reputation* "was actually a love story."[13] "End Game" sounds like a swaggering song, but it is about finding a forever love (guest Ed Sheeran sings about the Fourth of July party at Taylor's house where he connected with his now wife,[14] while rapper Future calls himself a "bad boy" but one who'll put his life on the line for you—ideal!). There's plenty of nervous energy on *reputation* about brand-new love: "Call It What You Want" and "Dancing With Our Hands Tied" are both fearful songs about losing the precious new relationship Taylor had started and which became her safe space during all the drama. When *reputation* was released, Taylor apparently told fans at the Secret Sessions that "Gorgeous" was about her "angel boyfriend of one year" and told them to spread the news.[15] When Taylor released entries from her diaries as part of the *Lover* deluxe edition, we learned that the relationship started late in 2016: an entry from January 2017 said, "We have been together and no one has found out for three months now."[16] The diary also showed how much Taylor wanted to keep the delicate new relationship quiet so it could grow, just like in "Dancing With Our Hands Tied": "I don't want anything about this to change or become too complicated or intruded upon."[17] Taylor's relationship with Grammy Award–winning songwriter William Bowery (for it was he) would inspire an eye-opening new type of Taylor song. "Dress" is so unexpectedly sexy that Taylor's parents apparently left the room when she played it at the Secret Sessions.[18] That's Andrea's baby!

There is a gift at the end of *reputation*: "New Year's Day." You don't often hear just Taylor at the piano on record: despite her rep for writing love songs, she's a popstar not a balladeer, and there's usually a driving rhythm. Here, the piano is alone in the background, just offset enough from the vocals to underpin them but not feel obvious. It's like Taylor and the music are comfortably pottering around the apartment, doing their separate tasks in harmony but not in unison. It sounds so simple, but it's surprisingly hard to play the piano line of "New Year's Day" and sing along at the same time. This isn't because we're in a wacky time signature (yet); it is in 4/4, which is so ubiquitous in pop it's called "common time." Time signatures are usually easy to find by clapping along with the vocal; this song has four claps per line, repeated four times. But just try clapping along with "New Year's Day" and you'll quickly get lost. This intimate, shambling song was a lifeboat for tender-hearted Swifties to cling to while bad-girl Swifties had the time of their lives. Taylor's natural gift for fitting strings of words to music is seeded here in a way we will see blossom on her most musically complex album, *evermore*.

It's the morning after the New Year's Eve party and there's glitter to be swept up. Songs like "Fearless" had focused on the exact moment the glitter is thrown and love is wonderful. Taylor said the final song on *reputation* was inspired not by the events of New Year's Eve, but rather what happens afterward: "I think there's something even more romantic about who's going to deal with you on New Year's Day. Who's willing to give you Advil and clean up the house."[19]

On New Year's Eve, resolutions are made for the coming year, and on New Year's Day we have to start keeping them. In the song there are references to storytelling and memories, but, unlike in most of her songs, Taylor's partner can read the pages of this story too, although she asks him not to skip to the end. In fact, she wants there to never be an end. She also entrusts him with something she has been holding on to all throughout her albums so far and used to fuel her songwriting: memories of their love. Her memory was all she could hold on to in "All Too Well," but it's not just her responsibility anymore; they can share it. This was the domestic kind of love Taylor had been wishing for in her daydreams, from "Mine" to "Stay Stay Stay." And her wish came true.

She also entrusts him with something she has been holding on to all throughout her albums so far and used to fuel her songwriting: memories of their love. Her memory was all she could hold on to in "All Too Well", but it's not just her responsibility any more; they can share it.

Taylor's *reputation* era was birthed from an awful time in her life, but, like many conflicts, it also provided a way to change: If everyone already thinks you're going off the rails, why not have that drink? In time, Taylor would come to value how it expanded our understanding of her as a whole person: "You've been cast as this always smiling, always happy 'America's sweetheart' thing, and then having that taken away and realizing that it's actually a great thing that it was taken away, because that's extremely limiting."[20] It's hard to remember now, but even seeing Taylor in streetwear was radical for someone who had always been pictured in pretty dresses or impeccable matching sets.

Not only does Taylor swear for the first time on "I Did Something Bad," *reputation* finds her drinking for the first time. Before, drinking was always portrayed as something out of control and unattractive: the critic in "Mean" ends up drunk at a bar, ranting about Taylor's singing. On *1989*, getting drunk was used as a metaphor for jealousy on "Blank Space," and wine was spilled on Taylor's dress in "Clean," a perfect way to end that album given the stain that would soon attach itself to her "America's sweetheart" persona. But on *reputation*, she drinks because it's fun. The video to "End Game" shows her drinking pints and downing shots in a rainbow-colored sequined dress. From now on, Taylor will mention drinking and getting drunk in a rich variety of ways in her music, including country music–style sad whiskey-drinking on "this is me trying" and champagne as a symbol of marriage on "champagne problems." Going for nights out is a normal way for a person in their twenties to spend time: most people don't meet their true love in their own backyard à la "Mary's Song (Oh My My My)" (*Taylor Swift*). Taylor will make drinking such a normal part of how she presents herself that from this point on she'll enjoy a glass of wine on talk shows and even ask for one in a commercial for a credit card company that sponsored the Eras Tour. It hasn't stopped her being considered a role model after all.

The early stages of dating are notoriously fraught— when can you declare yourself out of the dating woods and in a relationship? "Delicate" is a major entry in the "am I the girl from 'cardigan' or the one from 'august'?" (*folklore*) category of Taylor songs. Like in "You Belong With Me," Taylor knows that there are other characters in love stories beside the happy couple, including all the girls who didn't make it to girlfriend status but who still had big feelings. "Delicate" is the first sign that *reputation* could be a love album, and a corrective to the Taylor of "I Did Something Bad," who apparently doesn't care who she hurts because "everyone will betray you" (as she'll one day write on a blackboard in the video for "Anti-Hero"). Although she'll continue to offer dignity to the Augustines of the world, this time she is the lucky one. On *Red*, love and hope began again in a café, but now it's a dive bar.

Taylor is so renowned for her lyrics that we sometimes forget she is also the executive producer of her albums, crafting the sound. Anyone who doubts this should compare *Lover* to *Midnights*: they are produced by virtually the same set of behind-the-scenes people, but they don't sound alike at all. Taylor always makes sure that her songs paint the mood she wants to create through the sound, from dramatic strings on "Haunted" (*Speak Now*) to the persistent drone that expresses her inescapable anxiety in "The Archer" (*Lover*). Even at her most romantic, she usually makes the situation feel exciting with a beat, whether it's a tropical synth beat on "Delicate" and "Cornelia Street," or her own heartbeat on "Wildest Dreams" (*1989*). The lyrics in "Delicate" about the fragility of liking someone are emphasized by the use of a vocoder to make Taylor's voice sound extra ethereal. "Clean," the most introspective song on Taylor's previous album, *1989*, was produced by Imogen Heap, whose technique of layering heavily processed vocals can be heard on her influential song "Hide And Seek," where the fuzz at the edge of her voice takes on a quality almost like a church organ. "Delicate" is both ethereal and highly danceable. Taylor described the use of vocoder on the album's love songs as "really vulnerable and really emotional and really sad but beautiful."[21] "King Of My Heart" and "Getaway Car" also make use of the vocoder, and Taylor will call back to this in the distorted intro to "Midnight Rain" (*Midnights*).

The video for "Delicate" also showed, despite reports, that the old Taylor wasn't entirely dead. She goofs and pulls funny faces. When she finds herself on top of a car hood in a rainy back alley, the staple music video scenario, it's to show off her ability to do the splits, which she practiced for a whole year.[22] Taylor can be chaotic but, at the end of the day, she will always, always try. At the end of the video, where she's been on display for the paparazzi but simultaneously ignored by all the ordinary people working and staying in the hotel, she walks into a bar called the Golden Gopher, soaked from the rain as if she's run all the way there. Everyone turns around to look at her, but she's only looking for one person. Right at the end, she spots him, and Taylor's face lights up, golden.

7

What Really Matters

LOVER

On the last night of the Reputation Tour in November 2018, Taylor told the crowd, "I've been thinking a lot about the album *reputation*—I've always thought of this album as an emotional process of coping, it's like a catharsis."[1] The tour was a chance to have fun with it all, Taylor finding humor in the hardship she faced from her dramatic loss of public opinion: "I can't tell you how hard I had to keep from laughing every time my sixty-three-foot inflatable cobra named Karyn appeared onstage in front of sixty thousand screaming fans. It's the stadium tour equivalent of responding to a troll's hateful Instagram comment with 'lol.'"[2]

Hearing thousands of people sing along to her songs clearly influenced Taylor's next album, *Lover*, which she called "a natural continuation of events in my life" (wink-wink, smiley face).[3] A "love letter to love," it picked up the attraction that began in "Delicate" and blossomed in "New Year's Day" and turned it into a full love story. Taylor explained the difference between a crush and true love: "Are they honest, self-aware, and slyly funny at the moments you least expect it? Do they show up for you when you need them? Do they still love you after they've seen you broken? Or after they've walked in on you having a full conversation with your cats as if they're people?"[4] The ability to find things funny is romantic to Taylor: on *reputation*, the only truly happy moment is when she laughs during "Gorgeous," just after a line about her cats. Laughing is one of her vocal superpowers. From her first laugh bubbling up on "Hey Stephen," we've heard her laugh out of pure pleasure ("Stay Stay Stay") and cackle bitterly at the thought of forgiveness ("This Is Why We Can't Have Nice Things"). She laughs twice on *Lover*'s opening track, "I Forgot That You Existed," which is all about letting things go. Taylor described *Lover* as "open fields and sunsets and SUMMER,"[5] compared to *reputation*'s "nighttime, darkness, like, full swamp witch."[6] This fertile summer feeling hinted at the superbloom of creativity that would lead to her putting out two albums in a single year in 2020: "I really feel like I could just keep making stuff—it's that vibe right now. I don't think I've ever written this much. That's exhibited in *Lover* having the most songs that I've ever had on an album" (eighteen, to be exact).[7]

After years of uncharacteristic mysteriousness, Taylor was excited to stand in the daylight again, noting that the darker aspects she explored in *reputation* weren't within her natural comfort zone for connecting with her listeners.[8] This urge to connect means Lover is full of sing-along tunes and jauntier sounds. The planned tour was designed as festival-headlining shows mixed with Taylor's own mini-festivals. It was called Lover Fest and was going to feature lots of other acts alongside Taylor. One of the few public statements Taylor made during reputation was to release a Spotify playlist of songs she loved. She did the same for Lover, adding songs by The Chicks, Nicki Minaj, Kesha, and Clairo, among others. Rumors flew that these were the artists she would invite to play with her on Lover Fest, but sadly we'll never know, as the tour was canceled because of the Covid-19 pandemic.

Taylor was also ready to torment us with Easter eggs galore. The "Lover" video tells the story of Taylor and her boyfriend, played by her friend and backup dancer Christian Owens. They play out their lives, snuggling, partying, arguing, and making up, in a house with seven rooms, each with a distinctive color scheme. Seven rooms for seven albums!

1. A yellow-and-orange room where Taylor and Christian play board games on the ceiling—an Easter egg for the *Fearless* rerecord, which she was already plotting.[9]

2. A deep blue/purple room where Taylor plays a tiny piano alone until Christian joins her—creating songs all on her own means it's *Speak Now*.

3. A burgundy-and-cerise room where a New Year party is being held—all is well in the end, but the couple does have a conflict when Taylor thinks Christian is flirting with someone else. Taylor's party trauma is most evident on "The

Moment I Knew" and "All Too Well (10 Minute Version) (Taylor's Version) (From The Vault)" from *Red*.

4. A blue room where the couple swim inside a goldfish bowl. This could be a metaphor for media intrusion, explored in "Blank Space" and "I Know Places." It's *1989*.

5. A black-painted attic "up in the roof," like the moment in "King Of My Heart" when that guy wins Taylor by saying he fancies her. This is definitely *reputation*.

6. A pink room where the couple argue and make up. It's *Lover*.

7. A green room with a picture of a cat, where Taylor strums a guitar and plays drums. Her debut is the only album left, so it's *Taylor Swift*.

The house represents the domestic bliss Taylor had found, especially because it is inside a snow globe, echoing a line from one of Taylor's most tender romantic fantasies, "You Are In Love." It's also about the body of work she has built and the first hint that she is looking back across her eras (something she will add to on her Eras Tour, where she includes two more spaces in the house for *folklore* and *evermore*). Taylor said in 2019, "With every reinvention, I never wanted to tear down my house. Because I built this house."[10] Her next plan was to make sure she owned the house: "I've always written all my own music, I've always made all my own decisions, I've always curated absolutely everything about what I do, but you know, the fact that I own [*Lover*] just there's something about that that makes it more special than anything I've ever done."[11] *Lover* was joyful and goofy on the surface but it was also a serious milestone in Taylor's career: having signed a new record contract for the first time since her teens, it was the first album she owned outright.

When Taylor signed her first record deal in her Nashville days, she agreed, like most artists, that her label would own the master recording of her albums. In the olden days, this was a physical tape that held the original studio recording of a song or album from which all vinyl records, CDs, and eventually digital downloads were copied. These days, artists create digital masters, but the idea is legally the same: when we stream a song, it is a copy of the original master recording. This matters for two reasons: The money that is paid out when a limited-edition pink heart-shaped vinyl record is bought, or a song is played on the radio, is split into parts. Whoever owns the master gets a chunk of the money, and while some of that is passed on as a royalty to the artist, it could be a tiny amount, depending on their contract. The other chunk of the money goes to the people who wrote the

Lover was joyful and goofy
on the surface but it was also
a serious milestone in Taylor's
career: having signed a new
record contract for the first
time since her teens, it
was the first album she
owned outright.

song. You can see why a singer would benefit massively from writing their own songs and owning their masters. It's hard to make money if you're getting 15 percent of half of $0.01 per play from a streaming platform.

The other reason masters matter to Taylor is that they give the owner a vote, along with the songwriter, over what the music is used for. The owner of the master can decide if the song is used in TV shows, advertisements, or movies. When Taylor's record deal ended after six albums, her masters were sold by her old label. Now, the music that she'd written about her real-life experiences, from "Fifteen" to "Begin Again" to "Delicate," was being sold like it was merely a commodity. This made Taylor desperately unhappy as a songwriter and furious as a businessperson. On the suggestion of singer Kelly Clarkson, she began the process of rerecording her albums, with new covers and brand-new songs "from the vault." These "Taylor's Versions" have brought to light so many new songs and introduced the albums to new people who missed them first time around. The process meant Taylor spent time with her own incredible back catalog and inspired the theme of *Midnights* (13 sleepless nights from the past) and the entire idea of the Eras Tour. Taylor's joy and pride in somehow pulling off the labor-intensive process of rerecording her older music is clear: when releasing *1989 (Taylor's Version)*, the cover was the first one ever where Taylor is smiling. Kelly says that every time a Taylor's Version comes out, Taylor sends her flowers: "I got that really cute cardigan too."[12]

Taking control of her art gave Taylor her confidence back. In 2019, she solo directed a music video for the first time, for "The Man." *Lover* sounds playful, like in the bridge for "I Think He Knows," where the tune is almost audaciously close to a simple musical scale. Taylor felt liberated to do what she wanted in her new record deal: "The molecular chemistry of that old label was that every creative choice I wanted to make was second-guessed [. . .] I was really overthinking these albums."[13] Oh, and the bravado is back too: in "I Think He Knows," Taylor drives the car and, it's implied, the relationship. *Lover* feels rooted in the present day, with no worries about being timeless: there are funny references to other major 2019 celebrities and, after six albums of calling people on the phone, Taylor finally uses the internet to stalk her love interest in "Paper Rings." Although there's some pretend naivety on the album, Taylor's symbols are becoming more complex, just like her. Blue has been present in Taylor's lyrics from the start: on *Red* she looked into blue eyes; in "Gorgeous," on *reputation*, they were the blue of the ocean; and on *Lover* they've darkened to indigo. Blue has been connected to sadness and loss on past albums, but here it becomes an intrinsic part of love as they weather the ups and downs. In "Paper Rings," she'll jump into icy waters with him even if it turns her blue. In "Lover," his heart is blue but she wants it anyway, and forever.

While Taylor was previously quiet on her political views—something fans were disappointed in, particularly surrounding the 2016 presidential election—she used *Lover* to make her stance on social and political issues completely clear. What *Vox* called Taylor's "carefully crafted image of neutrality" had deep roots.[14] Taylor explained in the *Guardian* in 2019, "The number one thing they absolutely drill into you as a country artist, and you can ask any other country artist this, is 'Don't be like The Dixie Chicks!'"[15] The band now known as The Chicks had been huge in 2003, when a single political comment by their lead singer, Natalie Maines, led to a savage cancellation by a music industry that had previously worshipped them. One of the investors in Taylor's former record label, Big Machine, was country singer Toby Keith. He disliked The Chicks so much he performed in front of a banner with Natalie's face next to Saddam Hussein's. Theirs was one of the most notorious feuds in country music, and there's no doubt Taylor heard all about it in the early years of her career. The moment she severed ties with her old Nashville record company, Taylor invited The Chicks to sing with her, on "Soon You'll Get Better." Taylor found other ways to show solidarity with her fellow women in music: in a gesture of support for Kesha, she donated $250,000 to help the singer pay her legal expenses in the lawsuit brought against her by music producer Dr. Luke.[16] Speaking separately about the defamation case brought against her by a radio DJ who she accused of groping her, Taylor said, "Coming forward is an agonizing thing to go through. I know because my sexual assault trial was a demoralizing, awful experience. I believe victims because I know firsthand about the shame and stigma that comes with raising your hand and saying, 'This happened to me.'"[17]

Taylor tackled protest songs, a notoriously difficult genre, for the first time on "The Man" and "You Need To Calm Down." Threading the needle between a strong-enough statement and a catchy-enough song is tricky: the best political pop songs tend to engage with equality and self-empowerment inside a brilliantly euphoric package, like Lady Gaga's "Born This Way" or "9 To 5" by Dolly Parton. Dealing with the politics of elections and democracy in song is very different. For a start, how much can you assume the listener knows? In 2016 and 2017, many people felt like they were entering a conversation that had been going on without them for years, while people who were already invested in politics felt that these newbies were late to the party (kind of like being a *Midnights*-era Swiftie). Trying to catch up with this cultural change caused some significant pop music casualties. Taylor's peer in pop music, Katy Perry, had the 2017 single "Chained To The Rhythm," which argued that pop itself is a capitalist numbing agent designed to distract us from real-world events. The song was well crafted (a Max Martin joint effort, cowritten with Sia) and seemed to reflect Katy's genuine beliefs. It "spoke out" on politics. It has also become a milestone example of a creative risk and a well-intentioned statement hindering rather than enhancing a pop career.[18]

Taylor did her homework on politics as carefully and

The message that Taylor
sent by rerecording her
albums was that her work was
valuable, and by extension
so was she, and by further
extension so were her fans,
including all the young girls
in the audience.

methodically as she trained herself to do the splits: "I took a lot of time educating myself on the political system and the branches of government that are signing off on bills that affect our day-to-day life."[19] On *Lover* we can hear several years' worth of thinking on Taylor's part. Taylor's documentary *Miss Americana* gave fans an insight into how she has managed to weave activism into her day job as a popstar: "I want to love glitter and also stand up for the double standards that exist in our society. I want to wear pink and tell you how I feel about politics and I don't think that those things have to cancel each other out."[20] Taylor's biggest contribution to culture has been the way she has elevated pop music to the level of an art form (along with the equally influential Beyoncé). As she has gained the respect of the mainstream, so have her fans. Culturally associated with women and gay men, pop not only provides a rest from the burdens of life but a way to bond with others through hours of discussion and analysis. It only brings joy, and yet in the past it has been derided as shallow. The message that Taylor sent by rerecording her albums was that her work was valuable, and by extension so was she, and by further extension so were her fans, including all the young girls in the audience. The biggest political story of Taylor's career is that you should respect girls and their interests.

Lover's rollout was cut short by the events of 2020, but its story doesn't end there. There's a lot to choose from on the album, depending on your preference: the sultry saxophone-based "False God" sits next to "You Need To Calm Down." Taylor's performance of "False God" on *Saturday Night Live* converted many people to her music because it showed a different side to her from the radio singles they'd heard, from "Shake It Off" to "Me!" Even her outfit showed this was a new kind of Taylor: most of her fashion throughout the *Lover* era was bright, almost acidic colors and pastels. To sing "False God" she wore a chic black blazer and sequined flare trousers, a more glamorous, after-dark outfit. *Lover* has something for everyone. In a twist of fate, the new sound of country music held both "Me!" and "You Need To Calm Down" off the top of the Billboard chart: not even Taylor could get past Lil Nas X's game-changing TikTok juggernaut "Old Town Road." Another twist in the history of digital music came a few years later. The song that many fans think of as *Lover*'s standout track, "Cruel Summer," grew and grew in popularity, even throughout the *folklore* and *evermore* eras. It has the distorted vocals that have come to represent a kind of emotional vulnerability and uncertainty in Taylor's songs, but it also has a huge, catchy chorus and the most yell-able bridge since "Out Of The Woods." It's even got a callback to a Taylor classic, "Love Story," in the lyric about sneaking into a garden. The song's story recalls that desperate "Love Story" feeling too: "You're yearning for something that you don't quite have yet—it's just right there, and you just, like, can't reach it."[21] "Cruel Summer" waited for its moment, quietly getting more and more popular and creeping up the charts in the summer of 2023 as

Taylor toured and sang it as the first full song of the Eras Tour after a snippet of "Miss Americana & The Heartbreak Prince." In October 2023, it finally made it to the summit. Taylor, famously interested in numbers and making sure everything is present and correct, could relax: now every album she had put out since *Red* had its Billboard Hot 100 number one.

The Cats of Taylor Swift

TAYLOR'S FAMILY PETS

Before she had cats, Taylor was the joint owner of her family's two dogs, called Bug and Baby. They appeared in the vlogs Taylor posted early in her career and can be spotted in the video for "Christmas Tree Farm," which is made up of video footage from Taylor's childhood.

MEREDITH GREY

Taylor's first cat was Meredith, adopted in 2011. She is a Scottish fold and is named after Meredith Grey from the TV show *Grey's Anatomy*, one of Taylor's favorites. According to fans who met her at the Secret Sessions, Meredith is "soft as powder puff."[22] After a period of absence from social media (i.e. Meredith in her *reputation* era), Taylor was forced to address questions about her oldest daughter's whereabouts in 2021: "The truth is, Meredith just HATES having her picture taken."[23] Taylor used a picture of the introverted cat to promote safety during the pandemic: "For Meredith, self-quarantining is a way of life. Be like Meredith."[24]

OLIVIA BENSON

Olivia was born in June 2014 and is also a Scottish fold. She is named after the character Olivia Benson from the TV show *Law & Order: Special Victims Unit*; Mariska Hargitay, who plays Olivia, repaid the compliment in 2024 when she named her new kitten Karma. Taylor said, when picking names for her female cats, "Strong, complex, independent women. That's the theme."[25] Olivia travels in style: she was seen in *Miss Americana* being carried by Taylor in a special backpack with a window so she could see out. Olivia appeared in a Diet Coke commercial with Taylor in 2014.

BENJAMIN BUTTON

Taylor met Benjamin Button on the set of her video for "Me!" The cat handler told Taylor the kitty was available for adoption: "She handed me this tiny cat and he just starts purring and . . . he looks at me like, 'You're my mom, and we're going to live together.' I fell in love."[26] According to Taylor, Benjamin is prone to starting cat spats: "Benjamin always starts it and Olivia always finishes it. He's twice her size but she's an amazing fighter."[27] Benjamin had the special honor of appearing draped over Taylor's shoulders on her *TIME* magazine cover when she was named Person of the Year.

THE MOVIE *CATS*

"I have cats. I'm obsessed with them. I love my cats so much that when a role came up in a movie called *Cats*, I just thought, like, I have to do this. Like, this is my calling in life to do this—for the ladies."[28] In preparing for her role as Bombalurina in the 2019 movie *Cats*, Taylor began to understand her cats better by attending "cat school": "You watch these videos of cats, you watch them walking, you watch them sensing things, you learn facts about them anatomically, biologically."[29] The training paid off, because although the film failed to win any Academy Awards, critics and fans called out Taylor's performance as one of the few that understood the campy nature of the musical. Taylor said, "I had a really great time working on that weird-ass movie."[30]

KITTY COMMITTEE STUDIO

Taylor's home studio, set up to allow her to record vocals at home during the pandemic, is named Kitty Committee Studio. It has no fixed location and refers to wherever Taylor needs to record from home. The studio is named after the "itty bitty pretty kitty committee," Taylor's collective name for Meredith, Olivia, and Benjamin.

The Cats of Taylor Swift

"I have cats. I'm obsessed with them. I love my cats so much that when a role came up in a movie called *Cats*, I just thought, like, I have to do this."

Shout-out Song

"MISS AMERICANA & THE HEARTBREAK PRINCE"

When Taylor fled to a foreign land (the UK) during her retreat from the spotlight of 2016, she got the chance to look at America in the rearview mirror for the first time. Before this, American-ness was just the air she breathed: like many singers, one of her earliest public performances was singing the national anthem at a football game. However, the idea of coming to embody America was somewhere in Taylor's mind: before her Fearless and Speak Now Tours, the last song to play before the show began was "American Girl" by Tom Petty. Taylor's admiration for this song might be why she wrote "American Boy" for one of her very first demos in 2003, about a young man growing up in a small town.[31] As Taylor grew up, "American Girl" was replaced with "American Woman" by Lenny Kravitz for the Red Tour. Moving abroad only made her American heart grow fonder. In "King Of My Heart," she says her new boyfriend "fancies her," a sign she wasn't in Tennessee any more. On *Lover*, Taylor's familiarity with the UK comes through loud as day on "London Boy," with all its specific locations and Idris Elba's intro about riding a "scootah." After Taylor's love affair with England ended, she embraced her role as an all-American girl again, saying

"So Long, London" and swapping rugby matches for American football games. This brought her back within shouting distance of an important character in the story of America, and of Taylor Swift. Since *Fearless*, Taylor has invoked the ultimate symbol of American girlhood multiple times, and on "Miss Americana & The Heartbreak Prince" she brought her back, darker than ever: the cheerleader.

Way back in "You Belong With Me," the cheer captain was a rival for the all-important boy. When Taylor dressed up as a cheerleader in the video for "Shake It Off," it was one of the many inauthentic personas that Taylor tries and fails to embody. Clearly Taylor is never going to feel like the popular cheerleader, but she understands the cheerleader's symbolic power. In "Miss Americana & The Heartbreak Prince," the chorus is structured around cheer chants, making the cheerleaders (who shout "go," "fight," and "win") Taylor's backing singers. The song is set in a bleak version of the cute high school from songs like "Fifteen"—it's a song equivalent of the zombie Taylor from the video for "Look What You Made Me Do." Like zombie Taylor, the main character of "Miss Americana & The Heartbreak Prince" has lost her good-girl reputation: she even destroys her prom dress, a symbol of making it through high school. Instead, Miss Americana runs away, presumably never to graduate. It would be easy to believe it's a story song about the struggles of high-school girls, or a metaphor for the bullies of Taylor's *reputation* era, if she hadn't told us "it's definitely all about politics."[32] In writing "Miss Americana & The Heartbreak Prince," Taylor "wanted to take the idea of politics and pick a metaphorical place for that to exist."[33] From there flowed images like the homecoming queen, who wins a popularity contest that stands in for the presidential election. The subtext of the song is the desire to run away from all of America's problems, but Taylor can't do that anymore than Miss Americana can simply leave school. The song's claustrophobic feeling reinforces the context of *Lover* as a whole: engaging with politics often feels stressful and lose-lose, but it's no longer optional. Like "False God," "Miss Americana & The Heartbreak Prince" is written in the key of B minor, making it sound less bright and happy than tracks like "Lover" or "Paper Rings." These two minor-key songs leave us feeling uncertain and unresolved. In "False God," it's not clear if the love is true or false. In "Miss Americana

The subtext of the song is the desire to run away from all of America's problems, but Taylor can't do that any more than Miss Americana can simply leave school.

& The Heartbreak Prince," it's not clear if there is any way out of the cursed high school that is American democracy.

When it came to naming her documentary, which covered Taylor's disappointment at the critical reception of *reputation* and gave us insight into her songwriting process, she chose *Miss Americana*. This reflects the way that Taylor's life becomes national, or even global, news. To many people outside America, Taylor herself symbolizes the entertaining, spectacular aspects of American culture, as well as, unfortunately, the way that this culture treats its girls. The cheerleader is the ultimate American girl, but her sport isn't recognized or rewarded in the same way as male-dominated sports like football. The film's director, Lana Wilson, says they chose the title because, like the song, it looks at the dark side of the American girl: "Even if you don't know the song, I see the movie as looking at the flip side of being America's sweetheart."[34]

Into the Woods

8

FOLKLORE

*I*n the midst of a gray year, the message bloomed on a million phones: "she's doing something." Rushing to Taylor's Instagram, we saw a new set of square images, totally different in tone to all the previous ones, where glittery hearts were painted around Taylor's face or she posted cinnamon buns and cats. That day, there were nine black-and-white pictures of trees (TREES), with one grainy image of Taylor among them, wearing a huge, checked coat. There was no caption; she knew that we knew this could only mean new music. "She's doing something!!!!" one million people replied.

As a true albums artist, Taylor usually prefers an old-school rollout. She'll announce the existence of a new TS album either via social media (the *reputation* approach) or, more recently, at an awards ceremony in front of fans and other musicians. In August 2022, for example, she announced *Midnights* at the MTV Video Music Awards, and in February 2024, she used the acceptance speech for winning her thirteenth Grammy to announce her eleventh studio album, *The Tortured Poets Department*. Around two months' notice allows for hype to build, and singles and music videos to be released. With *folklore*, she casually ambled on to social media on July 23, 2020, and gave us sixteen hours to prepare ourselves emotionally, take a day off from our responsibilities, and find a nook to curl up into for uninterrupted listening. The next day, *folklore* was delivered.

When you wander through the trees, you find a whole "mythological American town" in *folklore*,[1] with a cast of characters from Taylor's life or imagination, including "a seventeen-year-old standing on a porch, learning to apologize. Lovestruck kids wandering up and down the evergreen High Line. My grandfather, Dean, landing at Guadalcanal in 1942. A misfit widow getting gleeful revenge on the town that cast her out."[2] There are addicts and exiles, teenage girls and health-care workers. Taylor also points out that there are many "lyrical parallels" across folklore, from her examination of the hard work it takes to be Taylor Swift on "mirrorball," to the hard work of being an addict and a recovering perfectionist on "this is me trying." These interconnecting points, all held together by Taylor's songwriting, the "invisible string" of all her work, make it a kind of mini Taylor-Verse in itself.[3]

Like everyone who went into lockdown in the early months of the pandemic, Taylor says she found herself utterly confused about what to do, if she should be doing anything at all.[4] But only for three days. Then she wrote folklore for something to do. As she faced life as a popstar with no stage, she thought of a fellow musician she had met back in 2019. Aaron Dessner, a guitarist and songwriter from the band The National, had told her that his songwriting process involved creating a track that he would email to his bandmates. Then they'd bat the song back and forth from wherever they were in the world. Taylor was used to sending voice notes with song ideas to her producers or receiving tracks from them to set her ideas to, but working entirely remotely instead of together in the studio was a new concept. Instead, sound engineer Laura Sisk, who has worked with Taylor since *1989*, came and set up a vocal booth in Taylor's wisteria-covered home in LA. Taylor christened it the "Kitty Committee Studio."

For the first time since *reputation*, the album's title and song titles are stylized with lowercase letters. Taylor said *reputation* "wasn't unapologetically commercial" and the same logic holds here.[5] *Folklore* was an experiment at a strange time, designed to be consumed in a low-stakes way. It's almost not a part of her popstar canon.[6] If it was too weird and people didn't like it, it could be treated like other popstars' mixtapes or genre experimentations and kept as a curio for completists. As a result, *folklore* has a playful quality: Taylor is like a (sad) theater kid, voicing all the different characters in Folklore-town. Many of the songs are structured more like snapshots, conversational Taylor songs in the "Treacherous" mode, punctuated by killer bridges. The more structured songs reach back to Taylor's country music training, with twists in "the last great american dynasty" and "betty" (the latter even has a harmonica for the full folk/country experience). The whole project feels as loose as Taylor's plaid shirts in the promo images. For the first time in her career, there was no huge business with hundreds of people's livelihoods revolving around her ability to have a hit song that led to sold-out stadium tours, or the internet bickering over whether she'd chosen the right single from the album or not. This music was just for her, and us, listening at home. So Taylor went to her musical home: Americana.

It's hard to put *folklore* in a box. Where some listeners heard alt rock, others heard a singer-songwriter record straight out of the 1990s (we have to wait until "willow" on *evermore* for Taylor to acknowledge the influence of nineties trends). The visuals were more DIY than usual due to lockdown rules, without full glam teams: "I'd be touching up my lipstick and then I'd run out into a field and [photographer Beth Garrabrant would] take pictures."[7] Although the sound is different, the Taylor album structure we have come to love is roughly intact: "the 1" resets expectations in the very first, sweary line; there is a heartbreaking track five in "my tears ricochet" and a light, youthful story song in "betty," in the Swiftian tradition of intentionally naive songs like "Stay Stay Stay." The subject matter is sadder, madder, and darker than on her previous albums, however. Taylor described the inspiration for "my tears ricochet" to Jack Antonoff during their gathering at Long Pond Studios to play the album through together for the first time: "Somebody could be your best friend and your

This music was just for her, and us, listening at home. So Taylor went to her musical home: Americana.

companion and your most trusted person in your life and then they could go and become your worst enemy, who knows how to hurt you because they were once your most trusted person."[8] Taylor will revisit this specific betrayal, which she describes as a blend of a friendship ending, a business backstabbing, and a bitter divorce, across *folklore*. She found that divorce stories, involving as they do the end of a shared mythology and the dissolution of a financial arrangement, chimed with what she was thinking about: "I wrote some of the first lyrics to that song after watching *Marriage Story* and hearing about when marriages go wrong and end in such a catastrophic way. So these songs are in some ways imaginary, in some ways not, and in some ways both."[9] *Folklore* explores complex emotions that Taylor has felt and hopes we might share: depression, unredeemed bitterness, the frustrated rage that builds up inside women across the years. They're expressed in the story of the much-criticized woman who used to own her house or Taylor's description of the shattering reality of trying to be everything to all people as a beloved fan idol. We learn more about who Taylor is from how she writes about these things than we could from a thousand tabloid headlines about her choice of man. It's not confessional, but intimate. *Folklore* is the most beautifully written conversation you could possibly overhear.

And what do we hear? Stories from the neighborhood. If we've seen one image crop up in both Taylor's lyrics and music videos, it's that she is always on the phone, from "Our

Folklore explores complex
emotions that Taylor has felt
and hopes we might share:
depression, unredeemed
bitterness, the frustrated rage
that builds up inside women
across the years.

Song" to "Maroon" via "Look What You Made Me Do." Let's listen in: "Did you hear young James went off with Betty in the end? I know!"; "That hussy Taylor Swift bought the Standard Oil house. Her Fourth of July parties are so loud"; "And did you hear her drop the F-word twice on this album? She's really lost her mind." Taylor's knack for balancing light and dark shows up when she swears. On "mad woman," she snarls, "Fuck you," while on "betty," James's concern that Betty might tell him to go fuck himself is far more lighthearted. Finally expressing anger is a major moment in Taylor's journey. Women's anger is commonly treated as insane and repulsive, as well as a loss of the moral high ground that is their only safety, so when popstars like Beyoncé express uncontained anger, for example in "Ring The Alarm," it's a major statement. Taylor's angriest songs pre-folklore are when she's able to take a moralistic stance, from "Should've Said No" to treating her nemesis like a naughty child on "Better Than Revenge" or "Bad Blood." The story of her broken relationship with people she had worked with from her earliest days, back when she was still dreaming about her songs being played on the radio, is murkier, involving contract negotiations and whispers around the music industry. Our main source of information is Taylor, and even she seems conflicted. Her tears "ricochet" back and forth between her and the antagonist—

this is an injury that wounds them both and a war that has no winners. "Mad woman" expresses her anger but also speaks to Taylor's right to sing about anything she wants. She made her first statement about feminism on "The Man," and now she explores the messy nuance of how the double standard makes her feel: "The most rage-provoking element of being a female is the gaslighting that happens, when for centuries we've been expected to absorb male behavior silently."[10] Taylor's version of events will not be rewritten: she has been putting abuse into words ever since the maddening chess games of "Dear John."

As well as addressing the quicksand (thank you, "Treacherous") of gaslighting, "mad woman" breaks new ground for finally using the word *woman* in place of *girl*. Pop is obsessed with youth and has a mixed relationship with adult women, as Taylor learned when she grew into one. Talking with *Vogue*, Taylor addresses the youthful ignorance she had of sexism as a teenager and how that flipped when she got older: "The second I became a woman, in people's perception, was when I started seeing it."[11] Taylor describes herself as a woman for the first time in "the last great american dynasty," which makes sense: girls are powerful in many ways, but they don't buy much property. The song tells the story of Rebekah Harkness, the former owner of Taylor's house in Rhode Island, where she holds her famous Fourth of July parties. The minimalism and spaciousness of Aaron's music inspired Taylor: "I had been wanting to write a song about Rebekah

Harkness since 2013, probably, and I'd never figured out the right way to do it because there was never a track that felt like it could kind of hold an entire story of somebody's life."[12]

This separation between girl and woman allows Taylor to write her most perfect and poignant document of innocence to date. The first three piano notes of "seven" rise up like the swing above the creek in Taylor's memory. She presses little-girl intonation into her voice on lines about braided hair and pirates, using her vocal instrument and her talent for adopting different voices to its best effect. The piano burbles along like it's being played by stubby, childlike hands. Some of Taylor's songs channel girlish energy, like "Stay Stay Stay" or "Love Story," but "seven" is more of a respectful testament to the seriousness of childhood interests; the little Taylor of the song has a full plan for helping her friend escape her angry father. The song also mentions the concept of a "folklore" of love, passed from person to person like a tradition or a folk song. Taylor once pulled from the images of love given to her, back on *Taylor Swift*. Now, Taylor creates new images of love, from cleaning up after the party in "New Year's Day" to this tiny, delicate portrait of two children walking along a creek, deep in conversation about running away to become pirates.

All these choices point to the genre of *folklore* being simply "Taylor Swift." But the genre has been debated across the press and fan forums because many people have an emotional stake in the categorization. Is the album "indie" or "alternative"? The label of "indie" originally described music made on an independent label rather than for a major record company such as Sony. Taylor and Aaron may have found common ground as Taylor was on an independent record label, Big Machine, for the first six albums of her career, making songs such as "Shake It Off" indie music by definition. Over time, "indie" has come to be associated not with how the music is distributed, but with a specific guitar-band sound, less heavy than classic rock and which explores more introspective themes, for example addiction ("this is me trying") and feeling sad. This met the tone of 2020 perfectly; as Taylor said about *folklore* and its enthusiastic critical reception, "everybody needed a good cry."[13] *Folklore*'s sound, and the presence of male indie musician Justin Vernon of Bon Iver, created some new paths into the Taylor-Verse for fans who did not feel comfortable walking down the fairy-light-strewn Girlhood Lane or encountering the crowds on Main Pop Girl Avenue. Aside from his indie credentials, Justin Vernon turned out to be a natural scene partner for Taylor. Taylor described hearing the bridge he wrote for "exile" as: "Hands on face, face is melting, everything is made out of confetti."[14] He went on to take a bigger role on *evermore*, playing guitar and drums on "cowboy like me" and the cranky poison-pen letter "closure," as well as helping us ascend to duet heaven in the wintry "evermore."

It may mostly do without pop-song drama (although the ending of "betty" has something in common with the twist in "Love Story"), but *folklore* isn't gentle. Somehow it disarms the listener and knifes them in soft places. In an acknowledgment, rare for pop music, of the specific experience of the Covid-19 pandemic, "epiphany" includes a reference to people having to hold their loved ones' hands through a plastic sheet for fear of catching the virus. Although Taylor had previously mapped out the darkness of lost love and taken strong political stands, it was still astonishing to hear her like this. It's a whole new Taylor mode. The new lyrical territory on *folklore* came from Taylor watching, listening to, and thinking about other people's stories as she sat and watched endless movies in quarantine. The beginning of "epiphany" even sounds like the slightly discordant jangle of an orchestra tuning up. The idea of hundreds of people gathering to perform and listen to music was just a fantasy in the summer of 2020.

That isolation may be why Taylor created herself a whole tortured high-school class to hang out with in the songs "betty," "august," and "cardigan." Listening to the album in order, we first encounter the main character of "cardigan," who has escaped the suburbs and the girl-next-door persona, and now wears "black lipstick" and "high heels." She's thoughtful and lyrical, imbuing her love interest with mystique and magic. If this boy really is James from "betty," Betty is doing a lot of work on "cardigan" to make him seem like a serious romantic figure (a meta-commentary on how Taylor makes her muses seem incredibly alluring and fascinating in her music).[16] In "betty," James is easily swayed by the girl from "august," named Augustine by Taylor in the *Long Pond Sessions*. The love triangle's crowning glory is the story of Augustine, the girl who spends one summer with James, and lives in hope that their fling will become a relationship. It's the type of situation Taylor describes on "Cruel Summer" and "Delicate": the tentative stages between hook-up and love, where you fear the person is on the verge of bolting. She looks down at his back when they go to the beach, longing to touch him and claim him for her own but not sure if she is allowed. James does bolt and Augustine is left with all this wasted time spent waiting for him to call. It's a kind and sensitive portrait of a figure who is usually left out of the story of love: the one who has their hopes dashed. Augustine is the "other woman," like the one in "illicit affairs." Taylor extends empathy toward these two women in a way that is often denied in a culture that considers adultery, in the words of "Getaway Car," the worst crime: "The idea that there's some bad, villain girl in any type of situation who takes your man is actually a total myth because that's not usually the case at all. Everybody has feelings and wants to be seen and loved."[17]

All those books Taylor was reading in quarantine crept into her songs. Throughout her work, Taylor has referenced lines of poetry, in and out of the lyrics: in the liner notes for *Red* she said that she was inspired by a line from Pablo

Neruda's poem "Tonight I Can Write": "love is short, forgetting is so long." "Illicit affairs" uses a literary reference to tie an invisible string back to a very old song. Taylor's 2006 song "The Outside," "illicit affairs," and "'tis the damn season" from her next album, *evermore*, all quote the Robert Frost poem "The Road Not Taken" and its famous final lines. It's a similar image to the parallel universe Taylor imagined in "The Man," where she wondered, "If I had made all the same choices, all the same mistakes, all the same accomplishments, how would it read?"[18] In "illicit affairs," the road less traveled is taken to avoid getting busted on their way to a secret meeting of the kind that the male villain of "mad woman" seems to have all the time (when Taylor plays it live, she counts off four or five flings on her fingers). This person cheats on his wife and she doesn't even seem mad about it, while Taylor went on a "normal amount of dates" as a young woman and to this day people's main piece of information about her is that she "has a lot of boyfriends."[19] The other path of "illicit affairs" is also an intriguing and generous acknowledgment of lives lived beyond the moral binary, where an affair partner can experience unique colors of passion, also used as a device for a unique connection in "Out Of The Woods" and "Question . . . ?" As Taylor explored on "Daylight," love need not be black and white after all, but red, gold, lavender, or blue. For an album with a monochrome cover, *folklore* ends up being a riot of color. In particular, she finds a new shade of blue in her palette. In "invisible string," "peace," and "hoax," Taylor mentions "the blues," or depression, as part of life and part of the person she loves. Talking with Jack Antonoff at Long Pond, she asked, "Who would you be sad with? And who would you deal with when they were sad? And, like, gray skies every day for months, would you still stay?"[20] She would stay.

The sun is setting on Folklore-town. When Taylor released the dreamy video for "cardigan," she was in a cabin, wearing a white nightgown and hair buns in the natural, wavy texture that would forever define this moment in her creative and aesthetic journey (as a result of social distancing, Taylor styled her own hair and wardrobe for the video). Like a scene from *The Lion, the Witch and the Wardrobe*, Taylor-style, she climbed inside a piano instead of a closet, finding a world full of stories inside. When *folklore* came out, it was received with the kind of rapture only a world of music fans who had been denied joy and novelty for three months could experience. It was unbelievable: not only was there a new Taylor album, but it took Taylor's songwriting to new places we couldn't have guessed existed within her mind. For Taylor, the love shown to the album was an encouragement to keep making music that wasn't directly tied to her celebrity: "I saw a lane for my future that was a real breakthrough moment of excitement and happiness."[21] In 2020, the future was still very unclear, and no one knew when a musician could be back on tour again. It felt like a small, quiet time when ordinary life was suspended. So Taylor decided she wasn't finished with this—*folklore* would have a sister.

Shout-out Song

"MIRRORBALL"

The quandary of how Taylor can appeal to all people, all the time, is explored on "mirrorball." Its imagery of the show coming to an end is pulled from Taylor's past tours, reflecting the disappointment of the canceled Lover Fest: the disco (*1989*), the rodeo (yee-haw, it's the Fearless Tour), and the circus (Taylor dressed as a ringmaster on the Red Tour) are all closed down. Speaking about writing the song in the midst of the pandemic, Taylor said it was "the first time, and one of the only times, that the time that we're living through is actually lyrically addressed . . . it's an album that allows you to feel your feelings and it's a product of isolation."[22]

When "mirrorball" was released, it already cut to the heart of Taylor and her drive to work even when she had every reason to rest during lockdown: "I have an excuse to sit back and not do something but I'm not, and I can't, and I don't know why that is."[23] The song has become more and more prescient as Taylor's fame has grown and we all come to terms with what it means to have our words and faces travel around the world via social media. Like Taylor's images of fame and the spotlight going all the way back to "Tim McGraw," it can be read two ways: "It was a metaphor for celebrity but it was also a metaphor for so many people [who feel] like they have to be 'on.'"[24]

As a celebrity and the icon of one of the biggest music fandoms, Taylor is the ultimate people-pleaser, pathologically set on creating fun album rollouts, entertaining hits, and, as she revealed in *Miss Americana*, maintaining a certain look in order to avoid criticism. Like all the tiny mirrors on the mirrorball, she's constantly creating new images of herself across platforms to make sure that we keep paying attention. It's a raw sentiment for a star who has cultivated such a close relationship with fans: fame can cut both ways. Talking about whether to even release "mirrorball," Taylor wondered if it was too raw.[25] For people who grew up with the internet, and especially for those who feel they have to be online for work or to find community, Taylor is also asking us to think about the toll that turning yourself into a brand takes: "Every one of us has the ability to become a shapeshifter, but what does that do to us?"[26]

The mirrorball shows us multiple versions of ourselves, and sadly it's not always our best selves. Over the past few years, fan culture has grown into a major cultural force. It's called the "fan economy" and it relies on our loyalty and devotion to particular people or brands. Taylor has proved herself to be one of our current age's greatest marketing geniuses, although it helps that she has an excellent product to sell: you can guarantee she will put out a high-quality set of songs every single time. In between album releases, she keeps our attention with tours; short film releases, like the one for the ten-minute version of "All Too Well"; and what writer Anne Helen Petersen calls her "gossip art," or the way she creates exciting moments out of something as simple as going out to dinner. Taylor is an exceptionally charismatic person, truly a sparkling mirrorball who lights up the room. But although she is superb at capturing our attention, she can't always control the results. Taylor's onstage plea in 2023 for "kindness and gentleness in our internet activities," so that fans would stop feeling aggressively protective over her, was largely ignored.[27] Exes, ex-friends, and music critics are all subjected to avalanches of nasty comments. It's a reflection of the mob mentality that can fester in any community, but it's frustrating to see in the fandom of a singer who values politeness so highly and whose most aggressive statement ever was "Better Than Revenge."

An increase in time spent on our phones in 2020 meant that more people than ever were on platforms like TikTok.

Taylor's onstage plea in 2023 for "kindness and gentleness in our internet activities," so that fans would stop feeling aggressively protective over her, was largely ignored.

Taylor's huge back catalog and intriguing personality made her ideal subject matter for everything from quizzes about how big a fan you are to true-crime-style deep dives from fans speaking straight to camera. The Easter eggs that Taylor had been planting all her career were the clues in the murder mystery, guessing at the next album release date was the solution and we were all Poirot. Taylor joined TikTok herself in August 2021, posting fun videos for us to scour for clues about the next album (a glitch in her video turned out to be a reference to the song "Glitch," from the deluxe edition of *Midnights*) and the kind of behind-the-scenes content we hadn't seen from her since before she vanished during her *reputation* era. The powerful narrative behind rerecording "All Too Well (10 Minute Version) (Taylor's Version) (From The Vault)" in November 2021 was a turning point. *Variety* reported that "in two days, views on TikTok content related to Taylor jumped from a previous high of 80 million to over 260 million as her fans discussed the new lyrics and tried to uncover the Easter eggs in the short film she directed starring Sadie Sink and Dylan O'Brien."[28] If Taylor was world-famous before, now she truly had her eyes set on the stars.

The Graveyard Shift

EVERMORE

*M*any of Taylor's albums open with a fresh start. On *1989*, Taylor's in a new city listening to a new soundtrack. When releasing *Lover*, Taylor made "I Forgot That You Existed" the opener, because she was just so over it. On *folklore*, Taylor really was on to new shit, sonically, creatively, personally, the whole carousel. But as exciting as reinventions are, they can also be taxing for her, as she described in her documentary *Miss Americana*:

> *Constantly having to reinvent, constantly finding new facets of yourself that people find to be shiny. Be new to us, be young to us, but only in a new way and only in the way we want. And reinvent yourself, but only in a way that we find to be equally comforting but also a challenge for you. Live out a narrative that we find to be interesting enough to entertain us, but not so crazy that it makes us uncomfortable.[1]*

When Taylor doesn't pour energy into a transformation, she can do the very best version of her current style of songwriting. On *Speak Now*, she wrote "Dear John" and perfected the Swiftian bridge. But even the *Speak Now* era involved designing a whole tour and doing tons of press. Taylor decided to keep making music with Aaron Dessner and Jack Antonoff the very day that they recorded the *Long Pond Sessions*. *Folklore* and *evermore* have a lightness because Taylor was taking time off from the day job of being a popstar, where "I need to make a tracklist where this one's for the stadium show, this one's for radio, this one's for people who want to get in their feelings, check, check, check."[2] Instead, Taylor produced storytelling masterworks like "'tis the damn season," heaving with imagery of small towns and trucks straight out of *Taylor Swift* but written with the benefit of fourteen years of honing her craft. And a few beverages: according to Aaron Dessner, after they filmed the *Long Pond Sessions*, "We played all night and drank a lot of wine after the fireside chat—and we were all pretty drunk, to be honest—and then I thought she went to bed. But the next morning, at nine a.m. or something, she showed up and was like, 'I have to sing you this song,' and she had written it in the middle of the night."

The new territory of these songs, exploring life outside "the one" (the mythical romantic partner, not the song) has drawn comparisons to folk singer Joni Mitchell, another all-time greatest songwriter about life and love. Joni Mitchell's mix of jaunty, upbeat songs full of sparkling detail, like the domestic harmony portrayed in "Chelsea Morning," and heartbreaking sad bangers like "River," make the connection between her and Taylor obvious. However, it had a bumpy start. According to the critic who inspired *Speak Now*'s "Mean," he was the one who suggested Taylor listen to Joni's *Blue*. No matter how she discovered the elder stateswoman of diaristic songwriting, by the Speak Now Tour, Taylor was smitten: she wrote Joni lyrics on her arms for five shows, including one with a very Swiftian lyric about

traveling down a lonely road, from "All I Want." While promoting *Red*, Taylor described *Blue* as her favorite album of
all time, because it "explores somebody's soul so deeply."[4]
Joni and Taylor have much in common as women in music,
not least being dismissed by some critics very early in their
careers, before their prowess became self-evident; a 1967
review of a Joni show described the future legend and
writer of *Rolling Stone*'s third-greatest album of all time[5]
as "an eyeful in a tight-fitting mini silver lamé dress, and
sporting flaxen hair that falls below her shoulders,"[6] while
a review of *Blue* in 1971 described it, hilariously, as "richly
contoured, beautifully singable songs, rather than anything more profound."[7] What more did they want?

Taylor has spoken of her admiration for how Joni has
"gone through so many shades of herself';[8] we definitely
saw new shades to Taylor on *evermore*. In
contrast to the sweet-as-sugared-almonds
imagery of earlier songs about marriage,
from "Mary's Song (Oh My My My)" to
"Lover," Taylor kills a murdering husband in
revenge on "no body, no crime (feat. HAIM)."
The jilted potential fiancé of "champagne
problems" takes the night train so he can
avoid judgmental eyes after his fiancée runs
away. "tolerate it" is inspired by English author
Daphne du Maurier's 1938 Gothic novel, *Rebecca*,
which describes tensions in the marriage of
the young (second) Mrs. de Winter. Taylor

says that when she read *Rebecca*, "I was thinking, 'Wow, her husband just tolerates her, she's doing all these things and she's trying so hard to impress him and he's just tolerating her the whole time.' There was a part of me that was relating to that because at some point in my life I felt that way."[9] After all the divorce energy on "my tears ricochet" and "mad woman" on *folklore*, it's a great couple of albums for commitment-phobes. If love is to be found, it's between two outsiders who meet under some kind of tent in "cowboy like me." One of Taylor's most spellbinding vocal performances, this slow, cinematic song from the perspective of a jaded female con artist is about meeting your match where you least expect it. Taylor's imagination is a great location scout: the song starts on a tennis court turned into a dance floor, passes through an airport bar, and ends up in the Gardens of Babylon.

Although *folklore* was a huge leap in sound, *evermore* contains the real boundary-pushing treasures. In "peace" on *folklore*, Aaron Dessner supplied Taylor with his most off-the-wall instrumental yet. It was a turning point. He told her, "When I heard you traced the bridge and that you traced all the weird timing and weird chord changes, it just felt like 'okay, we can do anything.'"[10] *Evermore* contains some of Taylor's oddest and most experimental music. The twisty time signature she hinted at trying out all the way back in "New Year's Day" comes to fruition in the unusual 10/8 time signatures in "tolerate it" and "closure,"[11] her most experimental song since she accidentally released eight seconds of white noise.[12] It's a real testament to Taylor's musical sense that she was able to write to such a complicated time signature. For those who track parallels between Taylor's artistic development and Joni Mitchell's, this is promising for Taylor's twentieth or thirtieth album, when she might do a jazz record, or write an opera, or turn her hand to any other musical genre she is interested in.

Taylor does in fact shine her light on opera in "marjorie," a beautiful song about her grandmother, the singer Marjorie Finlay. The lyrics relay the advice Marjorie handed down to Taylor about balancing cleverness with kindness, and politeness with power. It's fascinating to hear the impact of Taylor's maternal grandmother, who loved cold-water swimming and must surely be where Taylor has inherited her musical talent from: "She loved to entertain: At her parties, she would get up and sing for her friends."[13] Marjorie died around the time Taylor went to Nashville to try to hand out her demos. Marjorie didn't get to see her granddaughter's dreams come true, but she helped to get them started, taking Taylor to see her first musical, *Charlie and the Chocolate Factory*, which sparked the theater kid in Taylor: "I started doing kids' musicals, because I loved seeing these kids up there singing and acting."[14] We can see the long tail of this stage experience in Taylor's theatrical gestures onstage. There are moments in Taylor's music that she compares to "almost operatic" singing, like the belted *stay* in "All You

Had To Do Was Stay" (*1989*).[15] Now Marjorie lives on through one of Taylor's most touching songs about memory and regret: "I'd open up my grandmother's closet and she had beautiful dresses from the sixties. I wish I'd asked her where she wore every single one of them."[16] Marjorie's vocals, singing an aria from Puccini, can be heard in the background on the track.

Evermore has so many voices and musical contributions going on beneath the surface that it's a shipwreck full of treasure down there. We must acknowledge the dramatic string section in "Haunted" (*Speak Now*), but *folklore* was Taylor's first album to feature full orchestration, arranged by Bryce Dessner, Aaron's brother and fellow member of The National as well as the male voice you hear in "coney island (feat. The National)." The arrangements are even lusher on *evermore*. Forty musicians performed on *evermore*, compared to *folklore*'s twenty-one, perhaps because people had figured out how to use Zoom by that

Evermore has so many voices
and musical contributions going
on beneath the surface that it's a
shipwreck full of treasure down there.

stage of the pandemic. Justin Vernon's vocals add bass-y depths and a strained emotion in his higher register. They are embedded under Taylor's on "ivy" and "marjorie" and as a duet on the ethereal "evermore." In the song, Taylor describes memory as being like a paused tape—she can't move past a moment of loss. It's similar to the bonus track "right where you left me," where Taylor is frozen in time at the restaurant where her lover left her, as other people's births, marriages, and deaths zip past. In the bridge of "evermore," the layers of increasingly urgent vocals from Taylor and Justin Vernon represent "the clutter of all your anxieties in your head and they're all speaking at once."[17] Each line of "right where you left me" is stuffed full of words, giving Taylor barely a pause to breathe. These songs revisit the cycles of rumination Taylor struggled to escape on *1989*'s "Out Of The Woods." Given that she references being twenty-three, "right where you left me" could even refer to the same period of time. Finally, Taylor gives herself permission to leave in the deluxe version's final track, "it's time to go."

Memory is Taylor's number one all-time theme, and *evermore* is shot through with nostalgia for a past real or imagined: it's in the way Taylor retreads familiar ground with her hometown ex for old time's sake in "'tis the damn season," in the faded glory of Coney Island's amusement park and shopping mall, and in the dreams of her ex and his beautiful hair in "gold rush." Taylor gazes back at the past and reconsiders it in "happiness," sharing one of the most gentle and generous sentiments she has ever expressed. A soft church organ plays under her singing as if it's music for a memorial. She struggles with her bitterness at the end of a long relationship marred by deep hurts, hesitating, apologizing, and trying to take back her fury and jealousy. She looks to the future and the "new" Taylor, not because the old one is dead but because she believes she can live through this ending. There was once happiness between them and even time can never erase that truth. The song makes good on the grief and disbelief of heartbreak and is especially comforting for people who have found love and lived to see it end, which Taylor herself has. The simple forgiveness she offered to her exes by sending presents for their babies in "invisible string" was easy to give because she had a new guy. Here, she tries to offer forgiveness while still in the thick of her heartbreak and feeling insecure about being replaced. She also offers forgiveness to herself: this relationship might have ended, but, no matter what, there has been happiness in this world because of her.

Aaron Dessner described adding touches throughout the record to create a "wintry nostalgia,"[18] such as the sleigh bells that can just be heard on "ivy." It's notable that Taylor was starting the process of rerecording her first "Taylor's Version," *Fearless*, as she neared the end of recording *evermore*: "There were days when I'd be recording a song like 'You Belong With Me' then I'd be recording 'happiness.'"[19] As "it's time to go" says, sometimes endings

Memory is Taylor's number-one, all-time theme, and *evermore* is shot through with nostalgia for a past real or imagined.

can be the right thing for you: after the end of her record deal, Taylor was unfrozen and able to reclaim her music. Taylor considered *evermore* to be an album all about endings: "With *folklore*, one of the main themes throughout that was conflict resolution: trying to figure out how to get through something with someone [. . .] *evermore* deals a lot with endings of all sorts, shapes, and sizes. All the kind of ways we can end a relationship, a friendship, something toxic, and the pain that goes along with that."[20] In "champagne problems," an engagement is ended, while in "happiness" a long-term relationship has ended. In "no body, no crime (feat. HAIM)," several lives are ended. One of Taylor's clever approaches to songwriting is that she often looks for what isn't there (one of the most frequently used words in all her lyrics is *never*). *Evermore*, her album about endings, is the only one that doesn't actually contain the word *end* or *ending*. Throughout her whole writing career, she has been looking for happy endings and afraid of sad ones—think of how Taylor lives in fear of love ending and breaking her heart permanently in "Cornelia Street." On *evermore*, Taylor confronts the endings, and makes peace with them.

EVERMORE

Shout-out Song

"IVY"

In a speech to the Nashville Songwriters Association, Taylor explained that she had "secretly, established genre categories for lyrics I write. Three of them, to be exact. They are affectionately titled quill lyrics, fountain pen lyrics, and glitter gel pen lyrics."[21] Quill lyrics are for songs she was inspired to write "after reading Charlotte Brontë or after watching a movie where everyone is wearing poet shirts and corsets. If my lyrics sound like a letter written by Emily Dickinson's great-grandmother while sewing a lace curtain, that's me writing in the quill genre."[22]

The example Taylor gives for a quill pen song is "ivy," a song all about yearning and graves, and stuffed with references to literature and nature (as well as ivy and fields of clover, there is snowy winter weather that turns into spring). The use of words like *incandescent* led to Swifties developing what Taylor called "a really amazing inside joke where they're like: the starter kit for listening to *folklore* and *evermore*. And it's just a picture of a dictionary."[23] Then there are fountain pen lyrics, "modern, personal stories written like poetry about those moments you remember all too well," and glitter gel pen lyrics, which "are the drunk girl at the party who tells you that you look like an angel in the bathroom. It's what we need every once in a while." All the happy, upbeat songs in Taylor's catalog are glitter gel pen songs, from "Shake It Off" to "Bejeweled." It would be easy to assume that quill pen songs could never be hits, as they sound far too literary and flowery. But this is the person who wrote an eight-times-platinum satirical work on how the media treats women. We should never underestimate the power of Taylor to take an unlikely sentiment and turn it into a global smash, something she'd pull off on her next album.

For those who love the forest and witchy occurrences, "ivy" is peak *evermore*. The plucked banjo gives it a blue-grass/Americana sound we last heard on "Mean" (*Speak Now*). Taylor's song "Carolina" for the movie *Where the Crawdads Sing*, which is set in North Carolina, also uses this sound to conjure a picture of mysterious, swampy forests. This genre inspires Taylor to really sing. Her vocal on

We should never underestimate the power of Taylor to take an unlikely sentiment and turn it into a global smash, something she'd pull off on her next album.

"Carolina" is exceptional, with lush low notes and subtle use of the unique bluegrass technique of throwing the voice upward from one note to the next, like a very short yodel.[24] On "ivy," Taylor even does a rare—for her—vocal run, a short but complex sequence of notes fitted into a single syllable at the start of the chorus. Taylor has been a longtime fan of Americana, a genre somewhere between country, bluegrass, and alt rock, as shown by her collaboration with The Civil Wars on the song "Safe & Sound" back in 2012, which soundtracked a movie set in a dystopian version of a working-class American mining community, *The Hunger Games*. On the cover of the single, Taylor wears a diaphanous 1930s-style dress of off-white chiffon, which combines the look of faded cotton Depression-era dresses (as seen on Katniss and the other girls of District 12 in the movie) with a Gothic, ghostly look.

As well as including a reference to frozen hands, just like the ghostly "ice-cold hand" from the beginning of Emily Brontë's *Wuthering Heights*, and a quotation from a poem called "Compassion" by American poet Miller Williams, Taylor mentioned Emily Dickinson. One of America's most famous poets in the present day, Emily lived a reclusive life but quietly wrote stunning, passionate poems known for using hymn meter, a rhythm rooted in folk music, and dashes galore:

This is the Hour of Lead—
Remembered, if outlived,

As Freezing persons, recollect the Snow—
First—Chill—then Stupor—then the letting go—[25]

The story of "ivy," with its yearning for a secret lover, inspired fans to connect it to the story of Emily's life. Across decades, she wrote love poems addressed to her sister-in-law Susan Gilbert, including "One Sister have I in our house—" (1858) which ends with the words "I chose this single star / From out the wide night's numbers—/ Sue— forevermore!" Taylor has previously used the word *forevermore* in the distinctly un-witchy, un-Dickinsonian "Welcome To New York" (*1989*) and in "New Year's Day" (*reputation*), which mentions glitter and Polaroids (the opposite of Dickinsonian). For people who love the links between the stories of Emily Dickinson and "ivy," the connection was cemented when the song was used as the soundtrack to a love scene between a fictionalized Emily and Susan in the drama *Dickinson* in 2021.

The Stars Align

MIDNIGHTS

The lessons Taylor learned while writing *folklore* and *evermore*, as a person, as a celebrity, and as a songwriter, all came together on *Midnights*. Her deeply personal songwriting was a signature of Taylor's art and had brought her incredible success, but it was also exposing for her. This level of success didn't just mean love for her songs; it generated a spicy interest in everything from what restaurants she dined at to, of course, who she might be honoring with her time. Fame, which started out as a fun and playful way to promote her music and connect with fans, became a monster Taylor couldn't control. Intense scrutiny of her every word and action became exhausting: "There was a point I got to as a writer that only wrote very diaristic songs that I felt it was unsustainable for my future moving forward [. . .] On my bad days I would feel like I was loading a cannon of clickbait."[1] Taylor will have to play the celebrity game for the rest of her career, knowing that anyone she is seen with publicly will be added to articles listing every boyfriend she's ever had. But instead of becoming more reclusive, Taylor has actually become more relaxed and learned to enjoy the spotlight again. In her *TIME* Person of the Year interview in 2023, she said, "Yes, if I go out to dinner, there's going to be a whole chaotic situation outside the restaurant. But I still want to go to dinner with my friends. Life is short. Have adventures. Me locking myself away in my house for a lot of years—I'll never get that time back. I'm more trusting now than I was six years ago."[2]

No one could accuse Taylor of being calculated with the amount of loose, pleasurable chaos going on around *Midnights*. Taylor called it "a wild ride of an album," which she made with her buddy Jack Antonoff. In the past, Taylor has described working with Jack as "fully, fully acting on impulse and we're acting on intuition and we're acting on excitement and like, oat milk lattes." The tracklist for the new album was announced in a series of videos that Taylor called "Midnights Mayhem With Me," where she pretended to answer an old-fashioned phone and pulled bingo balls from a cage, each with a song title on it. In some of the videos, she held the phone upside down—what did it mean? Sometimes she held the phone in her left hand, sometimes her right—what did it *mean*?[4] A jumble of extra songs was dropped at three a.m. after the midnight release, which Taylor described as a "special very *chaotic surprise*."[5]

The unexpected success of *folklore* and *evermore*, which managed to be vulnerable without being exposing,

Taylor took a new approach to writing *Midnights*, less diary entry and more creative writing.

showed Taylor a way forward for writing songs that were personal without pointing a big neon arrow at her life for the media to follow (obviously, fans know how to join the dots). Taylor took a new approach to writing *Midnights*, less diary entry and more creative writing: "It's a concept album and the main question is: 'What keeps you up at night?' You could be up at night because you're reeling from having just met someone and you're falling for them, or you could be plotting revenge [. . .] If you think of that as like a creative writing prompt, which is what I did, that's where the album came from."[6] Taylor completed the concept album assignment like an A-plus student, mentioning the middle of the night in four out of 13 tracks on the main album and sticking to things that keep all of us awake: memories of the past, worrying what people think about you, plotting. The

On each track of *Midnights*, Taylor examines what fuels her insomnia: revenge, self-criticism, what–ifs about past relationships, and planning clever and devious ways to keep fans on their toes.

songs also sound like they belong together—unsurprising, given they are made by the same producer, Jack Antonoff, with extra help from Jahaan Sweet, Sounwave (who also collaborated with Taylor on "London Boy" for *Lover*), and Aaron Dessner on a small number of tracks.[7] Jack is a hugely important contributor for Taylor, not only providing friendship and a comfortable working environment, but crafting a sound that put her songwriting to the fore, starting with "Out Of The Woods." He produced much of Taylor's 2019 album, *Lover*, with help from Joel Little, the virtually silent man you see listening and nodding along to Taylor in the studio on *Miss Americana*.

On each track of *Midnights*, Taylor examines what fuels her insomnia: revenge, self-criticism, what-ifs about past relationships, and planning clever and devious ways to keep fans on their toes. One of the first things fans did was go through each track, connecting it to past times in Taylor's life and music to see which era inspired which sleepless night. Taylor has often been awake at the witching hour, from as early as "Our Song" on *Taylor Swift*, where she was speaking on the phone late at night with her boyfriend. However, there are only 13 specific mentions of midnights, or the middle of the night, on her first nine albums. These 13 songs make an extremely fun and representative Taylor Swift playlist:

- "You Belong With Me" (*Fearless*)—In the bridge, the boy drives to Taylor's house in the middle of the night, at which point she drops any pretense and says frankly that he should be with her, not that brunette girl from the video.

- "Untouchable" (*Fearless*)—A unique song in Taylor's discography: a cover version. Although the song was originally written and performed by the band Luna Halo, Taylor changed the melody and lyrics enough that she does have a cowriting credit. The middle of the night in "Untouchable" is for dreaming about love.
- "22" (*Red*)—In Taylor's first partying song, she eats breakfast in the middle of the night—she is *wild*.
- "All Too Well" (*Red*)—The middle of the night is for dancing around the kitchen.
- "Nothing New (feat. Phoebe Bridgers) (Taylor's Version) (From The Vault)" [*Red (Taylor's Version)*]— This duet with fellow singer-songwriter Phoebe Bridgers describes the fear that wakes them up at night: being replaced as music's hot new thing.
- "Better Man" [*Red (Taylor's Version)*]—Memories of lost love return in the middle of the night. The simply excellent "Better Man" was written for *Red* but eventually given away to country group Little Big Town. Taylor says, "I was either going to put on 'All Too Well' or 'Better Man,' [on *Red*] and then I left off 'Better Man,' and then later on, years later, Little Big Town ended up recording that song and it went to number one, it won CMA Song of the Year."[8, 9]
- "Style" (*1989*)—Sexy midnight.

- "You Are In Love" (*1989*)—More breakfast items are being consumed at midnight in this song, this time coffee. The dream lover wakes up in the night to tell Taylor she is his best friend. The low-key details included in the lyrics, from coat buttons to a photo of Taylor on her beloved's desk, to the snow globe that represents their perfect love bubble, connect to songs on *Midnights* like "Sweet Nothing" and "Lavender Haze."

- ". . . Ready For It?" (*reputation*)—Sexy midnight round two. Opens rep with the greatest throat-clearing in all art. The references to playing games are very "Mastermind."

- "New Year's Day" (*reputation*)—Closing out *reputation*, midnights are now a symbol of commitment, as Taylor wants all his midnights.

- "Daylight" (*Lover*)—Taylor says she no longer wants to be defined by the thoughts that plague her in the middle of the night. Then she carries on having thoughts in the middle of the night and writes a great album about them.

- "the last great american dynasty" (*folklore*)—A brilliant use of the hours of darkness as a place women aren't "supposed to be"—Rebekah Harkness's snobby Rhode Island neighbors gossip about seeing her outside her house, staring out to sea at midnight.

- "happiness" (*evermore*)—The memories of a long relationship that ended, including a dress Taylor once wore at midnight. There are lots of dresses in Taylor's earlier discography, although never one specifically worn at midnight before. From the party dress that represents Taylor's humiliating twenty-first birthday in "The Moment I Knew" [*Red (Taylor's Version)*] to the one bought only to be taken off in "Dress" (*reputation*), they are an important symbol in Taylor's work.

If we listed times Taylor was awake later than midnight, we would be here all day. She doesn't sleep—this must be how she writes and records so much music. The "3 a.m. edition" of *Midnights*, which added seven more tracks, was released just three hours after the main album and begs the question of why certain songs are on the main record and other ones dwell on the deluxe edition, other than Taylor wanting to release a 13-song album. Picking a tracklist, given that we've learned many songs end up in the vault, is tricky. When sequencing the tracklist for *Red*, Taylor said, "I wanted every emotion on the record to take up one slot . . . no matter what you're going through, if you need a song, you can find it somewhere on the record."[10] The strategy may be different from record to record, but the variety of upbeat and downbeat songs on each album definitely shows that Taylor values songs for different moods and even different kinds of fans. Limiting the album to 13 tracks in the era of streaming could be an emotional attachment to the classic album format, or related to physical editions, which have had a new burst of popularity as fans collect vinyl records and CDs—they have a limit to how many minutes of music they can hold. These days, we can play at being Taylor having to make these decisions. During the folkmore era, it became common practice for fans to create their own playlists combining songs from across the sister albums into one record, perfectly matching their own taste. The length of *Midnights* allowed for the same game, meaning fans could, just for example, replace "Snow On The Beach (feat. Lana Del Rey)" with, let's say, "Would've, Could've, Should've."

For such a sparkling and sunny person, Taylor seems to live in the dark on her songs. When we think of late at night in pop music, it's usually in the club. But Taylor's darkness is spent pacing the floor or staring out of the window. Precious things glow in the dark, from her lover's face in "Last Kiss" to love itself in "This Love" and "ivy." The potential for romance is high under cover of darkness: as well as plenty of sneaking around after dark in the early phases of relationships, like in "Cruel Summer," darkness creates privacy and intimacy. In "You Are In Love," her new love interest sneaks a look at her in a dark room. It's satisfying to see details from this song about Taylor's dream love play out in songs drawn from her life, so when someone touches her hand in a dark room in the bubbly "Gorgeous," we have to cheer for her! But Taylor's darkness is also more exciting and transgressive, like Rebekah Harkness roaming the cliffs in "the last great american dynasty," or the protagonist of "cowboy like me" waiting in the dark for her next conquest. In terms of the music, there's darkness in the very bones of *Midnights*. Taylor has always been careful to make sure her chord progressions aren't too odd and don't create any dissonance (where sounds jar against each other). When Imogen Heap suggested "a slightly 'odd' chord progression," when she and Taylor were writing "Clean," "[Taylor] quite clearly said, 'I think we're going to lose them at this point.'"[11] But when it came to writing "Vigilante Shit," Taylor used the musical interval known as the tritone, or "the devil's interval," which gives an unnerving sound to the music.[12] She hadn't reached for this spooky musical trick since she was mad at the whole world on "Look What You Made Me Do" (*reputation*). "Vigilante Shit" must be about someone she really, really doesn't like.

There's another kind of darkness emerging that balances Taylor's lightness: mental health struggles. Hinted at in the gray days of "evermore," she's frank on "Anti-Hero": she suffers from depression, like so many of us. Chart success isn't the most important thing when it comes to music, but "Anti-Hero" is a triumph because it is radio-friendly and fun to sing along to while also being weird as heck. Try explaining a song that puts the words *sexy* and *baby* together to your parents. Taylor has a real knack for writing songs that sound like the "pop beep" her haters love to criticize but are actually incredibly smart: think of "Blank Space" or "Shake It Off" and how they're media satires under the catchy hooks.

Although Taylor is as American as apple pie, she's popular across the world because her music speaks to people from all sorts of different musical cultures. Sometimes the marketing as well as the music hits different depending on whether you're listening in the US, Europe, or Asia. A quick quiz for British people: Which of Taylor's songs have been number one in the UK? Nope. Nope, not that one either. The answer is "Look What You Made Me Do," "Anti-Hero," and "Is It Over Now?"[13, 14] It took the comeback narrative around *reputation* to help Taylor crack the UK number one position. Taylor has also built fan bases in non-English-speaking countries where there is strong home-grown pop to compete with, such as Japan and China (Chinese fans call Taylor "Meimei," meaning "unlucky," because she struggled to make it past Adele and other artists in the English-language chart; Chinese Swifties are meimeis).[15] Taylor is the only American in the IFPI chart of the top ten bestselling global artists (although there are two Canadians, Drake and The Weeknd).[16] She has been both praised and derided for appealing so strongly to young women, but this kind of global success only comes as a result of making music that people from a huge variety of identities and backgrounds can enjoy. That's her true genius: the song that you listen to through your headphones and that becomes so personal can also touch something in the heart of a listener on the other side of the world, who has never visited New York in their life and has no idea what a screen door is.

Taylor was obviously very, very famous and successful in her previous eras, but *Midnights* changed the game. In January 2022, Taylor was averaging around 30 million streams per day on Spotify. She had finally overtaken the streaming heavy-hitters Drake and Bad Bunny, although she played cat and mouse all year with who would be more popular on any given day or month. It took until 2023 for her to be crowned Spotify's most-listened-to artist. By January 2024, Taylor was averaging 80 million streams a day on Spotify. In two years, she had boosted her listens by 50 million a *day*, just on one platform. She was still only halfway through the attention-grabbing Eras Tour. On top of all this success in streaming, Taylor still sells hundreds of thousands of physical records: Swifties love to collect the vinyl.

If you were googling Taylor-related things such as "that one Taylor Swift photoshoot" in 2024,[17] the search engine suggested the question "Why is Taylor Swift so popular all of a sudden?" Why indeed? The more traditional wing of the media finally realized Taylor was more than just a popstar: articles about her achievements started appearing everywhere from *The Atlantic* to the *Financial Times*. She was also putting in the work to be a mirrorball, using her celebrity prowess to promote the music in every possible arena. Taylor's fashion became noticeably more glamorous around the release of *Midnights*. To attend a record company party, she wore a deep blue, rhinestone-trimmed bustier dress with a huge white faux-fur jacket over the top, and sparkly platform sandals. This was a decisive end to the flannel shirts of *evermore*. But *Midnights* is not a string of bright, crisp diamonds, like a second *1989*. It's more like the moonstones she references in "Bejeweled": luminous but opaque. Although "Anti-Hero" and "Karma" are catchy, they don't levitate loud vocals over a laser-targeted beat, the way a maximalist pop album from ten years ago would. This album is a layered soundscape, with the ear-catching moments coming more from what Taylor says than an intentionally annoying pen-click or dramatic drop. Critics complained that the album didn't break new sonic ground, a curious stance given that Taylor's music has always stood apart from the current sound of pop to allow her songwriting to be the main story. The sound Taylor chose in 2022 was more lo-fi—*Midnights* is probably the first Taylor album you could study to.

This haze extends to how Taylor portrays love and life. There was a time when she would describe the tiniest details of someone she loved, from the color of their eyes to their "organic shoes." Although muses will obviously inspire different kinds of art—Taylor said, "I've never missed two people the same way—it's always different"[18]—there's a sense in *Midnights* that love is becoming a part of Taylor's universe rather than being the sun she orbits around. This was a natural progression for a thirty-something in a long-term relationship. Taylor wrote many songs about the "angel boyfriend" she found during her darkest times,[19] from the deeply romantic "Cornelia Street" to the virtually R-rated (for Taylor, anyway) "Dress" and "False God." His eye color was documented in "Gorgeous" (*reputation*), and we did hear about his love of rugby in "London Boy" (*Lover*), a song that sparked a UK-specific fan debate over where Taylor could have spent a night out in Brixton, South London. But across five albums, Taylor's partner becomes more and more abstract: "dazzling" and "magnetic" in "Lover," a glimmering "comet" in "Long Story Short" and finally "Sweet Nothing." This mysterious lightshow continues in the cosmic imagery across *Midnights*: after having stayed grounded in reality for so long, writing *evermore* seems to have unleashed Taylor's mystical side. Who knows what color her lover's eyes are in "Snow On The Beach," but they look like flying saucers. The coordinates for Taylor's star sign (Sagittarius, known for finding it hard to let things go) appear in the "Lavender Haze" and "Karma" videos. In "Mastermind," she's talking about stars and planets and fates aligning. Speaking of Taylor being a mastermind: the opening line from "Forever & Always" and "I Knew You Were Trouble" makes a third visit here, reminding us that all of Taylor's writing is her own story beginning "once upon a time."

Aaron Dessner commented when they were writing *evermore* that Taylor "writes a lot of songs, and then at the very end she sometimes writes one or two more, and they often are important ones."[20] Although Taylor wanted to craft a concept album of 13 songs on *Midnights*, she threw some paint at the wall with the "3 a.m." version. It's nearly an amazing full album all on its own. We got her shortest-ever song, "Glitch," which finally succeeds in making our wonderful, effortful Taylor sound casual about a relationship situation. "The Great War" adds violets, poppies, and morning glory to the flowers Taylor has mentioned in her songs. One song really stood out: the pained "Would've, Could've, Should've." Like "You're On Your Own, Kid," which revisits a past relationship with the furious eye of a grown woman, it explores how a teenager can feel drawn to a relationship with an older man even though it's damaging to her. The memories Taylor revisited in *Midnights*, in rerecording her albums and in arranging the Eras Tour, have uncovered a "tomb" full of ghosts who come out to haunt her on "Would've, Could've, Should've." With a frantic beat and agonized vocal, it's a portrait of regret and pain that once again looks at the negative space around a feeling: Taylor wonders who she would be if he hadn't looked at her, if she had stayed on the same trajectory. Life would have been less terrible and less wonderful at the same time: as she wrote in "happiness," she can't assign simple villain status to people who hurt her anymore. The song touches on the same sad reality as "All Too Well," that relationships can take away a part of you as easily as they can add to your life: Taylor misses who she used to be. A super-Swiftian identity was taken from her by this person: in the bridge, she sings a line about wanting her girlhood back, because it belonged to her first. It's staggering to hear about her losing, or having taken from her, the girlhood she wrote about with such tenderness and wholesome hope in her first three albums, the place where she was safe and free to daydream. The one comfort is that, as Taylor put it in her speech to the New York University class of 2022, "losing things doesn't just mean losing. A lot of the time, when we lose things, we gain things too."[21] Taylor's saddest songs are often the ones that other people find the most meaningful and comforting, and they are among her best work.

"Would've, Could've, Should've" is a new level of Taylor songwriting. At the same time, the rowdy "Hits Different," about drinking to forget your sorrows, shows she's still got breezy pop songs a-plenty. Taylor's mature career won't be defined by chasing chart relevance or succumbing to the inevitable hurts of a life well lived. There's going to be sunshine and midnight rain. The broad range of Taylor's talent makes it impossible to guess where she'll go next, however closely we look at her lyrics or track her every Easter egg. Luckily, at this point, we can relax. Only Taylor knows how the stars and planets and fates of the Taylor-Verse will align. We just have to follow her there.

The broad range of Taylor's talent makes it impossible to guess where she'll go next, however closely we look at her lyrics or track her every Easter egg.

Long Blond Sessions

Taylor is so closely identified with her blond hair that fans often call her simply "Blondie."

2006
Taylor uses her country music curls to emphasize her stage presence, performing dramatic hair-flips. Over the years, her hair has stopped forming a huge cloud of natural ringlets. Writing a list of thirty things she'd learned by the time she was thirty, Taylor said: "From birth, I had the curliest hair and now it is STRAIGHT. It's the straight hair I wished for every day in junior high. But just as I was coming to terms with loving my curls, they've left me."[22]

2009
Brief interruptions of Taylor's blond hair occur when she wears a straight black wig to appear in an episode of *CSI: Crime Scene Investigation* and to play the love rival in the "You Belong With Me" video. She often adds accessories such as headbands and butterflies to her hair in this era.

2010
Big news: Taylor straightens her hair and wore clip-on bangs to attend the American Music Awards.

2012

Taylor perfects her blond: not too pale, not too golden, just a perfect ashy dark blond. She wears a heavy bangs in the *Red* era, often with loose waves.

LATER IN 2012

Taylor briefly adopts a more emo-inspired look in the video for "I Knew You Were Trouble," sporting messy hair with pink ends.

2014

Hollywood glamour becomes an important inspiration for Taylor's red-carpet hair, for example the lavish waves she wears to the Met Gala in 2014.

2015

Taylor wears a red wig as her revenge-obsessed alter ego in the "Bad Blood" video.

LATER IN 2015

Taylor's haircuts are getting gradually shorter. She appears at the Billboard Music Awards with a wavy style that doesn't quite reach her shoulders.

2016

Taylor cuts her hair into a razor-sharp bob to attend the Grammys in February. In April, she bleaches her hair to go to the music festival Coachella. She captions an

Instagram photo "Bleachella," which becomes the official name of this look. Her new look is featured on the cover of *Vogue* and is showcased at the Met Gala, paired with a leather-and-silver cut-out dress and dark lipstick. This bleached look is referenced in "Dress" (*reputation*) as Taylor's current hair when she meets her new love interest, who has a buzz cut.

2017
Taylor appears on the cover of *reputation* with faintly wet-look hair. Her blond color is warmer and darker.

2019
Taylor dip-dyes her hair pink and lightens her shade of blond for the release of *Lover*. She wears various romantic hairstyles to events, including a braided updo.

2020
Fans experience Taylor's natural adult hair texture, a slightly crimped wave pattern, as she is forced to style her own hair due to the Covid-19 pandemic. Her *folklore* buns, worn in the video for "cardigan," instantly become one of her most classic hairstyles.

LATER IN 2020
The cover of *evermore* shows Taylor from the back with her hair in a long braid.

2021
Taylor appears in her self-directed video for "All Too Well (10 Minute Version) (Taylor's Version) (From The Vault)" wearing a red wig to match the naturally red hair of the actor who plays her in the video, Sadie Sink.

LATER IN 2021
Taylor's hair is very long, and often worn with a side-swept bangs. She embraces her natural wavy texture for day to day and tends to wear her hair styled to one side, Hollywood-style, for events.

Long Blond
Sessions

MIDNIGHTS
Shout-out Song
"YOU'RE ON YOUR OWN, KID"

Taylor described the whole of *Midnights* as a "collage,"[23] and one song acts as three minutes and fourteen seconds of collage cut and pasted from Taylor's life. "You're On Your Own, Kid" gives an alternative take on everything we've seen Taylor go through, in her music and in public. Her innocent earliest crushes, which we heard all about on *Taylor Swift*, are now repainted as boys who would rather smoke than show up at the party, leaving her hanging around aimlessly looking at other people who she thinks have a "better body" than her. At this point, she's still the good girl of "Sad Beautiful Tragic," who says she'll wait and wait. It's the beginning of a painful series of growing-up moments and realizations, finishing on a cliff-hanger ending.

As Taylor grows up in the song, she isn't waiting around at high-school parties anymore, but hosting them. Her problems don't get easier, though: having the best body is now central to her career. This culminates in the rawest line she's written yet, about starving herself. Public scrutiny made Taylor feel pressure to maintain a low weight: "When I was eighteen, that was the first time

I was on the cover of a magazine. And the headline was like 'Pregnant at 18?'"[24] In *Miss Americana*, Taylor talked about the toll this took on her, leading her to "just stop eating." In the following lyric of "You're On Your Own, Kid," Taylor says she thought true love's kiss could save her. She wrapped the carrot and stick of femininity into two lines: "if you can be thin enough, you'll find love, and if you find love, your life will be saved." Taylor may have believed this back when she asked Romeo to save her in "Love Story," but lately she's been her own hero, or maybe anti-hero. As well as the person she used to be, there is also a reminder of the songwriter she used to be, nestled there in the melody: a perfect T-drop.

"You're On Your Own, Kid" rewrites the love stories Taylor has always told and shows what was previously just offstage in those narratives: her career and her search for herself. As Taylor comes to publicly own her "business" side, she puts her career choices into the songs because she's proud of them, even when the decisions were difficult. One boy in "You're On Your Own, Kid" could have persuaded her to stay in her hometown. Maybe, for true love, she should have stayed? (No.) Taylor has described love as good, bad, difficult, real, ruthless, brave, and wild. There's no doubt she's the laureate of love songs. But although she finds endless inspiration in it, that doesn't mean she is obsessed with it to the exclusion of all else. Even during the release of *1989*, Taylor had a positive outlook on single life and, taking it further, even embraced the loneliness that has defined her career and persona from the earliest days of being an excluded teenager who just wanted to connect, to the isolation of being the world's preeminent mirrorball. She gave *Rolling Stone* this incredible image in 2014: "Have you heard of the Loneliest Whale? [. . .] It has a call unlike any other whale's. So it doesn't have anyone to swim with. And everybody feels so sorry for this whale—but what if this whale is having a great time? Because it's not bad that I'm not hopelessly in love with someone. It's not a tragedy."[25] When she turned thirty, Taylor told *Elle* that she would no longer let external opinions influence how she lived her life and ran her relationships: "For an approval seeker like me, it was an important lesson for me to learn to have my OWN value system of what I actually want."[26] "Lavender Haze" makes it clear that Taylor will enjoy love without pressure to act like a 1950s housewife, thank you very much. It could mean maintaining a relationship while going on an epic tour that takes her away from home for months on end. It means choosing her own partners and running her relationships in a way that works for them, not for headline-writers, or even for fans. There are also other kinds of love that Taylor cherishes. *Midnights* is teeming with references to friendship, but "You're On Your Own, Kid" has a special lyric that has taken on an even greater meaning.

In her wise and generous New York University commencement speech, which she made five months before *Midnights* was released, Taylor said:

My experience has been that my mistakes led to the best things in my life. And being embarrassed when you mess up is part of the human experience. Getting back up, dusting yourself off, and seeing who still wants to hang out with you afterward and laugh about it? That's a gift. The times I was told no or wasn't included, wasn't chosen, didn't win, didn't make the cut . . . looking back, it really feels like those moments were as important, if not more crucial, than the moments I was told "yes."[27]

This is the Taylor who can write the bridge to "You're On Your Own, Kid," about loss and burning bridges. She has learned from these experiences and now wants to live in the moment, not just in the past. She suggests a way of feeling and tasting the present moment: making friendship bracelets, an image packed with girlish delight and love for your friends as well as classic Taylor earnestness. If you love your friend, make matching bracelets to cement your love forever! You could also send them sugar cookies or a present for their new baby, like Taylor does.

Although fans had been giving Taylor friendship bracelets at meet-and-greets and secret sessions for years, the lyric turned the habit into a cultural phenomenon. Fans started making armfuls of bracelets to wear to tour dates, to be swapped with others for a lasting memory of both Taylor's performance and the communal experience of being a Swiftie. The most perfect element of this practice is how people immortalize their favorite lyrics and Taylor moments in their bracelets, an ever-changing living museum dedicated to Taylor's work and Swiftie enthusiasm. Long titles have to be turned into acronyms, which brings a puzzle-solving element to figuring out what this nice girl from Row F is trying to swap with you—what does ATW10MVTVFTV mean?[28]

Taylor gets hyped about friendship, including her relationship with fans, because she didn't always find it easy to make friends. In "Mastermind," she puts her constant planning down to a childhood in which the other kids didn't want to play with her. School wasn't easier: "Even as an adult, I still have recurring flashbacks of sitting at lunch tables alone."[29] But after going all-in on her friendship with a celebrity "girl squad" during the *1989* era, she realized that she might be overcompensating: "Other people might still feel the way I did when I felt so

Taylor gets hyped about friendship, including her relationship with fans, because she didn't always find it easy to make friends.

alone. It's important to address our long-standing issues before we turn into the living embodiment of them."[30] These days she seems like someone you would invite to your party and it wouldn't matter how anyone looked or who was famous and who wasn't. You could look back on your past mistakes, even Bleachella,[31] and laugh about them, and she'd have a big glass of white wine with ice cubes in it, her favorite.[32]

Jack Antonoff said that Taylor wrote "You're On Your Own, Kid" before his eyes in the studio. They recorded it, and that was it. They didn't push the song into a classic structure with a final chorus or give it a "Love Story"–style happy ending. She finds perspective on her life in "You're On Your Own, Kid," but she doesn't rewrite history and say it's all okay. These experiences were sad and they hurt her. But isn't that life? This ambiguity, and the song's empathy for all the Taylors past and present, makes it the track that most encapsulates *Midnights*.

Spinning in Her Best Dress

TAYLOR ON TOUR

"Hi, I'm Taylor!"

When Taylor was twenty years old, she said, "I'm never more motivated by anything than I am by the sound of screaming people. That's my favorite sound in the world."[1] After three albums that had no tour attached, Taylor finally made her triumphant return to live music on March 17, 2023, in front of 69,213 screaming people.[2] Huge fluttering pink chiffon fans parted to reveal Taylor rising from beneath the stage, singing "Miss Americana & The Heartbreak Prince." The crowd went wild. The Eras Tour had been five long years in the making. Those who had got into her music during the pandemic were yet to experience their first Taylor tour, including their first example of Taylor introducing herself as if her reputation didn't precede her. For those who had cried when Lover Fest was canceled, it was a chance to finally hear live versions of beloved songs like "Me!" For those who had been to every tour, this was a chance to relive memories and see how Taylor would reinterpret their old favorite songs. Would Taylor bring back her habits from previous tours, like writing lyrics on her arm, doing a heart shape with her hands, and bestowing her hat on a lucky crowd member? (Spoiler: At least one of these.)

The tour is jaw-dropping. Every night creates a new cultural moment through surprise songs, when Taylor plays tracks she couldn't quite squeeze into the setlist. Even though Taylor plays for up to (and sometimes longer than) three hours, she has more than two hundred songs to choose from. Concert-goers desperately hope to hear their niche personal favorite when Taylor slips the acoustic guitar strap over her head or sits down at the piano covered in hand-painted flowers.

After all it has been through, *Lover* finally gets its moment to shine. The fabulous pink-and-blue sparkly Versace bodysuit Taylor wears for the *Lover* section that opens the show was even the image used to promote the Eras concert movie. The movie was a huge smash all on its own. It was, appropriately, number 22 in global box office takings for 2023, despite only coming out in mid-October. *Lover* has the range to open the show: "Miss Americana & The Heartbreak Prince" leads into "Cruel Summer," which has the energy to get the party started and helps everyone get their vocal cords warmed up. Taylor has elected not to perform "Me!" although live performances have sometimes

For those who had been to every tour, this was a chance to relive memories and see how Taylor would reinterpret their old favorite songs.

SPINNING IN HER BEST DRESS

helped make sense of songs that weren't originally as well liked on the album: the Reputation Tour was known for transforming people's understanding of the record, which was divisive when it first came out. The crowd finally gets to sing "The Man," "You Need To Calm Down," and "Lover" together, as Taylor always intended, with "The Archer" perfectly rounding out the section.

The next section of the Eras setlist is *Fearless*. Unlike *Lover*, this did have its very own tour (2009–10), Taylor's first opportunity to headline. A little Taylor tour history helps to understand what's special about her live show. Before Taylor headlined her own tour, she had gone out on the road as the support act for country singers like George Strait and country music royalty Faith Hill and Tim McGraw. Her first big chance came when singer Eric Church was fired as the opening act for a Rascal Flatts tour. Taylor wrote in her diary in October 2006, shortly before *Taylor Swift* came out, "OH MY GOD I am on the Rascal Flatts tour! I got the call yesterday and I screamed louder than I can ever remember screaming before."[3] When Taylor stepped in, Eric joked to her that she should send him her first gold album, which she later did, with a note that read, "Thanks for playing too long and too loud on the Flatts tour. I sincerely appreciate it."[4] These country tours taught Taylor some useful lessons about playing live, particularly from George Strait, who was known for being soft-spoken. Taylor said: "The challenge with a stadium show is making those people in the very top row feel like they got an intimate, personal experience [. . .] I don't like to scream at the audience, I like to talk to them."[5] To this day, Taylor doesn't yell like a rock star; she talks to the crowd as if she's talking at a dinner table: "When I'm doing a concert, it's not like, 'WHAT'S UP LONDONNNNN!' I pretty much just speak at this level."[6]

George was also known for performing "in the round," with the stage in the middle of the venue rather than at one end like in a theater. Many singers have adopted this setup now so more fans can get closer to the stage. On the Fearless Tour, Taylor would even go backstage and run through corridors to the back of the arena. During the run, a joking clip played on the video screen, showing various men whose name Taylor had apparently included in a song. They included actors from her music videos and Tim McGraw, who sighed, "People forget that I was actually the very first victim of a Taylor Swift song."[7] Then, suddenly, Taylor would run up the stairs of the exit and surprise fans who thought she would be a distant dot for the whole show: "There's a B-stage at the end of the arena, so for part of the show the best seats in the house are what you used to think are the worst seats in the house. Ha! Switcheroo."[8]

Sometimes, in all the discussion of her songwriting talent, we forget that Taylor is one of the world's greatest performers as well. Her voice has strengthened since 2006, and she now has the experience, the budget, and the team to pull off a seamless stadium show. But her special charisma has always been there. She wanted to be a star so much that a songwriting deal wasn't enough for her, and rather than hang around in development hell in Nashville, she left her recording contract. That's the miracle of her: she has a Nashville songwriter's heart paired with a businesswoman's mind. The singer Carly Simon, who wrote "You're So Vain" (one of Taylor's favorite songs), said, "I wouldn't compare her to Joni Mitchell, Carole King, or me. Onstage she's a showman, sort of like Elton John."[9] Looking to the world of pop for the first but not the last time, Taylor brought dancers on to the Fearless Tour to enhance the storytelling element, an unusual move for country music. During "Love Story," Taylor would disappear behind her dancers and then burst forth in a wedding dress. Then she would pull the crown from her head and bestow it on a lucky fan. As the concert-goers screamed her name, Taylor gushed, "You guys . . . you have no idea what you just did for me."[10]

Fans had a motivation to scream at Taylor's tours—word spread that the "most over-the-top Taylor fans" in the crowd would be hand-picked by Andrea, Taylor's mother, and brought backstage for a "T-party," the private meet-and-greet later called Club Red, Loft 1989, and finally the Rep Room. Taylor's meet-and-greets were legendary; she once held a session that began at eight in the morning and ran until nine at night (13 hours). As well as putting in the effort with fans, Taylor treated her band like friends. Some of her band members had been with her for three years by the Fearless Tour, and some still play with her today, or came back on the rerecorded versions of *Fearless* and *Speak Now*. In 2009, her staff already numbered 150 people; Taylor was the CEO of a business. On the very last date of the Fearless Tour, Taylor graduated from arenas to stadiums. She played Gillette Stadium in Foxborough, Massachusetts. The venue has been a staple on Taylor's tours ever since she became the first woman to headline a concert there.

When Taylor returned to Gillette Stadium for her Speak Now Tour, she created a piece of Swiftie history. On June 25, 2011, "the rain show" happened during a storm, but Taylor kept dancing in her best dresses. "Fearless," "Last Kiss," and "Dear John," three songs that explicitly mention rain, were all performed in the downpour. On her next visit, during the Red Tour, Taylor told the crowd, "I thought, 'Oh my god, they're all gonna leave,' [. . .] and guess what you guys did? You stayed and you danced and you got even louder."[11] Taylor called it "one of the most memorable nights of my life," because it could only have happened live on tour: "It's those moments of human interaction that happen on tour that you can't get just watching a song climb the charts, sitting in your house."[12]

The Speak Now Tour (2011–12) took what made *Fearless* so entertaining live and took it up a notch. The entertainment factor was slicker: during one of Taylor's costume changes, a dancer performed a tap dance, then approached an outsize light switch. When he flipped it, Taylor popped up from beneath the stage like a jack-in-the-box. Taylor said, "I really like for there to be something theatrical about what we do onstage. When I was younger, I was just obsessed with Broadway shows. As much as I can show these audiences an element of that theatrical nature to a performance, I think that it allows them to escape from their lives a little bit more."[13] The show did feel more like a play, with multiple stage sets including a B-stage with a glittering tree and a gold pergola. In some ways, *Speak Now* is peak Albums Taylor, at least until *folklore*, and so the tour opened not with an upbeat sentiment about being ready to party but a soliloquy on regret that is so her: "Real life is a funny thing. I think most of us fear reaching the end of our life and looking back regretting the moments we didn't speak up. When we didn't say I love you. When we should've said I'm sorry."[14] For "Our Song" and *Speak Now*'s "Mean," Taylor appeared in the kind of ethereal white vintage dress that had a grip on fashion bloggers in the early 2010s. Vintage dresses even made their way into the lyrics of "Better Than Revenge," not that it helped the song's antagonist: in the live show, the song was introduced with a fake voicemail message saying, "Hey, it's me. Leave me a message and make it hot," in a Valley-girl accent. Taylor's *Speak Now* footwear was black knee boots, moving away from her previously established country image and into Americana territory. Though Taylor kept a hint of her country roots when the banjo came onstage during "Mean," it was clear in this moment that being part of the country music scene was in Taylor's past and would only live on in certain songwriting styles and the occasional harmonica.

Other casualties on Taylor's tours were some people's favorite songs, as until the Eras Tour she kept only a handful of songs from previous albums on the running order, preferring to play as much of the current album as possible. Slower songs tended to fall by the wayside, apart from "All Too Well." "Dear John," considered one of her most iconic songs, was played on March 2, 2012, toward the end of the Speak Now Tour, and wouldn't be heard again until Taylor played it as a secret song in 2023, shortly before *Speak Now (Taylor's Version)* was released. The Eras Tour has only two songs from *Speak Now* on the setlist: "Enchanted," for its romance and girlhood ties, and later "Long Live," the adopted fan anthem.

Surprise songs have long been an important part of how Taylor makes a stadium show feel cozy. On the Speak Now Tour, she played surprise cover versions, ranging from "A Sorta Fairytale" by singer-songwriter Tori Amos to "Lucky" by Britney Spears. The Red Tour (2013–14) was where Taylor first played surprise songs from her own catalog. By the Red Tour, Taylor was becoming concerned about not being entertaining enough, so she brainstormed how to create an even better time for the audience: "My generation was raised being able to flip channels if we got bored. We want to be caught off guard, delighted, left in awe."[15] She began bringing out surprise guests with a connection to the city, including country star Luke Bryan in Nashville, or Ed Sheeran in London, who was also the first surprise guest of the 1989 Tour (2015).

Ed Sheeran's influence can be seen in the way Taylor chose to cover her own song "Blank Space" on the 1989 Tour. She had already been giving the crowd fresh versions of songs to create a special live experience, such as a sixties girl-band version of "You Belong With Me" on the Red Tour. For her reworked version of "Blank Space," Taylor used looped audio of herself shouting the name of the city she was in to create a unique version for every stop of the tour. Other personalized moments have included the bespoke T-shirts with the current city's name on it that Taylor wore throughout the Red Tour. Costumes also leveled up on the Red Tour: the pretty dresses of *Fearless* and *Speak Now* were replaced with cleaner silhouettes and a more grown-up look. Taylor even opened the show with a Beyoncé-style outline of herself projected on to a curtain, the mark of an icon in the making. Taylor's beautiful gowns became less prom dress and more golden age of Hollywood; she wore an Alexander McQueen dress with exaggerated hip embellishments to sing "I Knew You Were Trouble," an exciting high-fashion twist on the white wedding dresses of previous tours. To press the point home, she executed a reverse "Love Story," vanishing behind her dancers momentarily and emerging in a sparkling black bustier and micro-shorts, though she did keep a *Fearless* gesture, taking the black felt hat from her head and giving it to a fan during "State Of Grace."

Fast-forward to the Eras Tour and, at the end of "22," one lucky fan gets to come right up to the stage and say hi to Taylor and receive her hat. The *Red* section of the Eras Tour uses the album's bops—"22", "We Are Never Ever Getting Back Together," and "I Knew You Were Trouble"—to raise the energy; sensible, as it is the midpoint of the show and comes just before the emotionally charged *folklore* section. The exact midpoint is the move from "I Knew You Were Trouble" to the ten-minute version of "All Too Well." When Taylor first performed this song, she looked sad and troubled. Over time, the audience's reaction would transform how Taylor felt about it in a remarkable process of healing:

> *This song was born out of catharsis and venting and trying to get over something and trying to understand it and process it [. . .] You turned this song into a collage of memories of watching you scream the words to this song, or seeing pictures that you post to me of you having written words to this song in your diary, or you showing me your wrist, and you have a tattoo of the lyrics to this song underneath your skin. And that is how you have changed the song "All Too Well" for me.*[16]

The last tour before Eras, the Reputation Tour (2018), acted as a form of processing on a larger scale. As she did no interviews for the album, it was where Taylor got to express herself directly to fans. Hearing how good the music sounded live and seeing Taylor perform onstage without inhibitions helped people who initially didn't receive the album enthusiastically come to appreciate it. Taylor said, "*Reputation* was interesting because I'd never before had an album that wasn't fully understood until it was seen live. When it first came out everyone thought it was just going to be angry; upon listening to the whole thing they realized it's actually about love and friendship, and finding out what your priorities are."[17] Every show on the Reputation Tour took Taylor one step closer to rehabilitation in the public eye. Eventually, it would become a record-breaking success, and Taylor's first tour entirely in massive stadiums rather than smaller arena venues, helping her reach an overall attendance of 2.9 million people.

The set design for the Reputation Tour was inspired, building on the spectacle Taylor had been crafting during her pop career. *Red* had its cleaner, clearer vision, and *1989* went full spectacular, with light-up bracelets handed out to audience members in some territories, creating a magical sparkling cosmos across the venue. The bracelets changed color and pulsed to the beat of the music, adding yet another element to the 360-degree sensory overload designed to whisk you deep into the Taylor-Verse for a few hours. *1989* was Taylor at the height of her pre-*reputation* popular-girl moment, and the tone was pure entertainment. The Reputation Tour stage set was more ambitious but created a very different atmosphere. The backstory that inspired *reputation* was right there on the stage in the form of fifty-foot snakes. It wasn't the first time Taylor had referenced her public image onstage. During the Fearless Tour, she had her "victims" video and a skit of her being interviewed about her famous boyfriends, culminating in throwing a talk-show host's chair off the stage. During "The Lucky One," on the Red Tour, she had dancers dressed as 1940s paparazzi. In 2014, Taylor hired her publicist, Tree Paine, to help manage her image, an increasingly complicated and demanding job. The Reputation Tour had a more complex message to convey than "websites run a lot of stories about me": Taylor

Hearing how good the music sounded live and seeing Taylor perform onstage without inhibitions helped people who initially didn't receive *reputation* enthusiastically come to appreciate it.

had metaphorically died and come back to life. Taylor gave *reputation* everything she had, especially with her dancing. There was strutting, but, like in the "Look What You Made Me Do" video, she also threw her hips around for the first time. Taylor has always expressed herself mostly with her hands, but she incorporates more dance into the Eras Tour: "I had three months of dance training, because I wanted to get it in my bones. I wanted to be so over-rehearsed that I could be silly with the fans, and not lose my train of thought. Learning choreography is not my strong suit."[18] The dancing in Eras is just right: less pop-girl choreography and more storytelling, just as Taylor intended back on her Fearless Tour. She also incorporates tiny details from her own dance past, such as the carefree spinning around she used to do as a country artist. The office setting for "The Man" is pure musical theater, while for "willow" Taylor's dancers waltz with glowing orbs in a witchy ritual.

Folklore and *evermore* were the albums that Taylor wrote when she didn't have to plan for a tour, so it was intriguing to see how they would work in a huge stadium. In the end, Taylor had a clear vision. She had already described how the songwriting for these albums was a highly visual process, like the imagery of "mirrorball": "I immediately saw a lonely disco ball, twinkly lights, neon signs, people drinking beer by the bar, a couple of stragglers on the dance floor—just sort of a sad, moonlit experience."[19] The *evermore* section of Eras comes right after *Fearless.* The growth across twelve years is incredible to witness as Taylor pairs her sophomore album with her most musically complex record to date. "Love Story" is an eternal classic because it tells such a compelling story, but "'tis the damn season," "Marjorie," and "champagne problems" cover greater expanses of emotional ground and reveal more of Taylor's skill. Juxtaposing these two sections makes us wonder where she'll go given another twelve years. The imagery for *evermore* also illustrates the Gothic elements of the album, with video projections of deep, dark forests. It's a spooky setting straight out of *Grimms' Fairy Tales*. In an extra nod to this inspiration, for most shows Taylor wears a dark yellow dress with a lace-up bodice, channeling old-fashioned European wench-wear.

Folklore, which is sandwiched between the pop-oriented *Red* and *1989* sections, has one of the show's most memorable sets. The moss-covered-cabin stage set, inspired by the "cardigan" video, was first seen in Taylor's performance at the 2021 Grammy Awards. It is the stage set for seven full songs from *folklore*, plus a spoken-word version of "seven." For this section, Taylor wears an ethereal floor-length chiffon gown with cape-like sleeves that emphasize dramatic flings of her arms. This is especially good for lyrical, contemporary dancing along to "august," the song which inspired thousands of dramatic TikToks in the summer of 2023, or for singing the bridge to "illicit affairs" like an avenging angel, her chiffon wings streaming in the wind. Luckily for us, these songs sounded good in a stadium as well as in our headphones.

After the surprise songs section, Taylor nonchalantly walks to the middle of the stage. The floor appears to have turned into the rolling waves of the ocean. Suddenly, she dives right into the water. Fans sitting up high, in those supposedly worst seats, get an incredible view of Taylor "swimming" all along the stage and right to the giant video screen at the back. She appears again, climbing a ladder into the clouds, ready to get lost in the "Lavender Haze." It's a gasp-out-loud moment of stagecraft and surprise. By this point, Taylor has been onstage for over three hours. This is the kind of performance that opera singers give, or star athletes, and Taylor is somehow still going strong. She trained hard for six months to have the stamina for the show, and to improve how her vocals sounded when she was dancing: "Every day I would run on the treadmill, singing the entire set list out loud," she said. "Fast for fast songs, and a jog or a fast walk for slow songs."[20] When, after three hours or more, she arrives at the summit of this Everest of a show, "Karma," it is a moment of triumph.

The Eras Tour is legendary because it has impacted the world in ways beyond even Taylor's imagination, especially through the sheer energy of the fans. Taylor has a powerful strut, but even she couldn't single-handedly create a 2.3-magnitude earthquake like the one fans set off in Seattle through the sheer intensity of their dancing. The friendship-bracelet phenomenon has meant fans can spend time crafting in anticipation of the show and score a bespoke memento from other fans on the day. Making costumes is a fun part of going to any major event, from your friend's Halloween party to the *Barbie* movie, but few events give you the equal opportunity to dress as a fairy princess, a zombie, a witch of the woods, a marching band leader, or a mirrorball. You can show up to Eras in a sundress and cowboy boots, or a black hoodie, or just red high-waisted shorts and a striped T-shirt. Before long, people started arriving in perfect replicas of Taylor's new stage costumes, from the *Lover* bodysuit to the spangly, beaded *1989* crop top and miniskirt. In a perfectly circular moment, like karma coming back around, one fan went *as* a friendship bracelet.

Seeing Taylor live is a special experience: not only is the atmosphere dazzling, overwhelming, and joyous, it can never be repeated. Together, Taylor and her crowd sing their hearts out to create a unique, shared moment centered on the tall person in a sparkling bodysuit but made up of every single person in the crowd. In every show, Taylor struts to the end of the long, narrow stage, right out into the middle so everyone can see her, even up in Row Z. She takes a bow, flicks her hand in a theatrical gesture, or spins in her high heels, the light sparkling on every facet of her rhinestones. It's what she was born to do.

A people's History of Taylor Swift

12

THE FANS

*O*nce upon a time, Taylor caught your eye. Maybe it was a music video, or a song played at a party, or something in the news that piqued your interest. One by one, Taylor has welcomed us into her universe, and we've made it our home. She's shown herself to be a fearless leader in the music industry, a musician of incredible depth and versatility, and an endlessly fascinating celebrity. She works tirelessly to entertain the world with new music, incredible shows, gorgeous outfits, intriguing celebrity friendships—all a delight to watch and talk about with your friends. Taylor must have caused a billion hours of conversation, one for each of the dollars she's earned from her music.

Taylor fans are willing to spend so much of their hard-earned money on their love of their favorite artist that it has been called "Swiftonomics." It's fun to own a little piece of the Taylor-Verse to put on the shelf, whether it's heart-shaped vinyl records or one of the album-cover blankets some fans have collected since the earliest days. Taylor has sparked a renaissance in vinyl record sales, helping them reach their highest sales in the UK since 1990, when Phil Collins was the bestselling album artist.[1] In the US, vinyl now accounts for 72 percent of all physical format sales.[2] Physical formats are important because artists make more money from them, but also because you can't hang the digital-streaming version of *evermore* on your wall. Imagine if one day the internet went down and you couldn't listen to Taylor (consider memorizing all her songs just in case electricity goes down too). Vinyl is the best because it's bigger than a CD: a CD would look ridiculous propped up in your aesthetic work or study space. That's why rare vinyl is so sought after. A vinyl record of *Red* sent out to Academy of Country Music Awards voters, with the words "One of Nashville's finest exports . . . and she painted the ~~town~~ world RED" is for sale on Discogs.com for $5,999.99 at the time of this writing. Cheaper alternatives include the translucent orange *reputation* vinyl (the color is believed to hint at a lost album between *reputation* and *1989*) for $1,000 or, of course, *Midnights*, which is widely available in colors such as lavender and moonstone blue.

T-shirts with Taylor's face on them have been available for every era, for the fan who isn't afraid to announce their Swiftie identity to the world. For a more subtle nod, Taylor's 2019 collaboration with British designer Stella McCartney

It's fun to own a little piece of the Taylor-Verse to put on the shelf, whether it's heart-shaped vinyl records or one of the album-cover blankets some fans have collected since the earliest days.

(of "London Boy" fame) featured a T-shirt with a picture of her cat Benjamin Button. It takes a serious fan to recognize one of Taylor's cats. Although headlines often focus on how much money Swifties are willing to spend on their love of Taylor, it is not necessary to have lots of money to be a fan. A key feature of the Swifties is creativity. Fans often craft their own DIY merch with witty artwork that even Taylor's T-shirt designer can't compete with. Some of the best cross genres, just like her album *Red*. You can buy a shirt that spells out Taylor's name in a thorny font so it looks like you stan a death metal band called Taylor Swift. An Instagram user called @hiscissorsaurus designed a T-shirt that depicted Taylor and one of her cats in sunglasses, in a parody of indie band Sonic Youth's album *Goo*. You could even make yourself a replica of Taylor's Junior Jewels T-shirt from the "You Belong With Me" video, with your own friends' names or all the album names.

Getting involved is a signature part of being a Taylor fan, and one of the most enjoyable. Going to the Eras Tour was a blast for those who could get tickets, but for those who couldn't go, there were other ways to get on the hype train. In the US, fans gathered in stadium parking lots to listen to the booming music, hang out, and have a free dance. Going to see the Eras concert movie in theaters became an experience; Taylor posted to specify "Eras attire, friendship bracelets, singing, and dancing encouraged."[3] Renting the movie at home was a stealthy way to convert siblings and parents to Taylor and raise the chances of them buying merch for you as Christmas gifts. Club nights that play *only* Taylor songs have popped up across the world, from Taylor Fest in the US to Swifty Nights in Europe and Swiftogeddon in the UK. If you're lucky enough to live in the major Swiftie hub of Manila, Philippines,[4] you can catch drag queen Taylor Sheesh perform an Eras-themed show at the mall.

If only equipped with a phone, you can watch the concert through livestreams from fans with Taylor-level arm stamina, or just check out the secret song performances. Many Swifties have made videos using Taylor songs and attracted a like or a comment from Taylor herself on TikTok. In the *1989* era, talking about Taylor online could even score you an invite to her new invention, the Secret Sessions: "I would go online and I would look at their Instagram pages or their Tumblr or their Twitter," a practice known as "Taylurking."[5] In an act of incredible trust, fans were invited to Taylor's house, where they ate home-baked pumpkin-chocolate or coconut-chocolate cookies. Taylor, like an ambassador, knew everyone's names. She always pays close attention: fan Mikael Arellano was amazed to see his viral dance to "Bejeweled" incorporated into Taylor's performance of the song on tour in 2023.[6]

Taylor has kept up these gestures throughout her career because she was once a fan too. When she met her idol LeAnn Rimes as a kid, "she was going around and shaking hands with people in the audience, she looked down and I was like, 'LeAnn, did you get my letters?' and she goes,

'I sure did, Taylor!' And that was the moment where, literally, it all just clicked for me, that if I could ever make one little kid feel that way, or one person feel the way she made me feel, then it would all be worth it."[7]

Swifties as a collective like to discuss everything about her work in detail. When Taylor does something—anything— fans scour it for clues called **Easter eggs**. These give an indication of something she might do next, or gesture to the meaning behind a song. Taylor has been scattering these Easter eggs from her very first record: "Why not capitalize random letters and see if the fans figure out that if you take all the random letters and you put them together, it spells out little codes, secret messages?"[8] Getting a new Taylor CD between the years 2006 and 2014 was all about tearing the cellophane off the compact disc you'd bought at the record store and settling down with a pen and paper to figure out the secret messages. The very first hidden message, for "Tim McGraw," was "Can't tell me nothin'" (Lil Nas X is a known Nicki Minaj stan rather than a Swiftie, but his country song "Old Town Road" does feature a lyric very similar to this). The last ever hidden message, for "Clean," also featured in the video for "Out Of The Woods": "She lost him, but she found herself, and somehow, that was everything." Hunting for the clues helped fans notice just how poetic the lyrics were, and they started to build out a universe from the songs themselves: "It makes people read the lyrics, it makes an album more of an event. Easter eggs are a way to really sort of expand the experience of seeing something or hearing music."[9] *Reputation* didn't have secret liner note messages, but Easter-egging in her visuals became a major hobby for Taylor:

> I wasn't doing interviews, and so I still wanted to be able to communicate messages to the fans. So the Easter eggs really went into overdrive. I think the most Easter-eggy video of my entire career thus far was "Look What You Made Me Do." It will be decades before people find them all.[10]

There's no evidence that she cackled maniacally after giving this quote, but she definitely reveled in it. Unsolved Swiftie mysteries from this video include the version of Taylor who saws the wing off an airplane and sprays "reputation" on its side; she isn't recognizable from any video, tour, or era. Mysteries like this sit in Taylor's vault of secrets alongside all her diaries (and probably the scarf). When it comes to what Taylor wears, particularly to big events, certain colors can be used to send clues: "Easter eggs can be left on clothing or jewelry" or "a specific way you can leave Easter eggs is on nails [. . .] I did a Spotify vertical video for 'Delicate' [*reputation*], and I painted my nails the exact color tones that I wanted the next album [*Lover*] to be."[11] Taylor thinks of her favorite lyrical or visual symbols as Easter eggs too:

These are things that may not lead to something in the future, but they're just a tribute to my love for them. Those things are 13s and cats. If you see a cat in symbolism in my Easter egg situation, that's just because I love cats. It's really that simple. Sometimes it means nothing other than just reminding you how much I love cats. Also the number 13—really close to my heart. I will pick dates, I will pick really important dates, just because the number of those dates add up to the number 13. It rules my life.[12]

Fandoms are not all sunshine and rainbows, even if we wear them on our Eras costumes. Sometimes admiring Taylor goes very wrong. In September 2015, the rock-oriented singer-songwriter Ryan Adams released a cover record of *1989*. Yes, the entire album, song by song. He conducted a de-slayification process on this iconic pop album, taking away the beats and changing the pronouns so no one would get confused between Ryan and Taylor. *Pitchfork*, an indie magazine that hadn't reviewed Taylor's *1989*, gave Ryan's Version a 4 out of 10 and said: "there's no essential reason for it to exist."[13]

Even the fun of Easter eggs can go awry. Taylor has raised expectations so much that sometimes we see things that aren't there: When Taylor posted a picture of herself behind a fence with five holes in it, in February 2019, fans began to obsess.[14] Was it a countdown? This time Taylor just wanted to post a pretty picture: "I really just was trying to change up my Instagram aesthetic to get ready for the new album." Later in the year, she posted the picture again, five days before *Lover* came out: "Okay NOW there are five holes in the fence."[15] Taylor is a major public figure, so it's natural that fans will pay close attention to her actions and have opinions on what she does. She has said herself that she hates it when people can't handle any criticism and tries to stay open to it, which has even resulted in some close friendships:

Hayley Kiyoko was doing an interview and she made an example about how I get away with singing about straight relationships and people don't give me shit the way they give her shit for singing about girls—and it's totally valid [. . .] But I can't really respond to someone saying, "You, as a human being, are fake."[16]

Taylor has been called fake ever since she first looked at a screaming crowd in wide-eyed amazement. But sometimes people insinuate that Taylor's whole life is a lie. A significant subculture within many fandoms, not just Taylor's, is the theory that a celebrity is secretly gay (not to be confused with queer fans making personal interpretations of Taylor songs). Theories such as "Gaylor," which argues that Taylor is keeping her sexuality a secret, are an important part of fandom for some people who enjoy thinking about Romeo and Juliet–style forbidden love. Taylor has said she finds attempts to "sensationalize or sexualize" her female friendships uncomfortable.[17] In 2024, the internet chitchat bubbled over when the *New York Times* ran a 5,000-word opinion piece arguing for the Gaylor theory.[18] The article tests the boundaries of who can call themselves a Swiftie: Would you attempt to out someone you love in the *New York Times*? Some fans also take it upon themselves to overload the social media of people they suspect of hurting Taylor with comments and emojis, ironically doing exactly what people did to Taylor in 2016.

If we can maintain respectful boundaries with Taylor, the possibilities we can find in her music and celebrity are endless. Writer Emily Yahr has called Taylor "a portal into endless subjects: artistry, songwriting,

Somehow, Taylor makes being
a fan feel personal.

production, capitalism, race, gender, feminism, fandom, social media."[19] Taylor's music is a friend: it makes the good times even better and offers comfort when life gets tough. It's especially important that she illustrates the pain of heartbreak, because it can shape a person's life. It's vital to acknowledge the experience is valid and to be able to spend time feeling your feelings. Somehow, Taylor makes being a fan feel personal. A fan and avid collector of Taylor merch, Molly Swindall, summarized the feeling in an interview with the *Washington Post*: "She's always been so good with her fans and so caring, and I think that's why she's as big as she is. I understand she doesn't actually know me, but she makes you feel like you know each other [. . .] I stayed by her through every single era, through all the thick and thin. And that's something that I get to be proud of: that whether it was cool or not, I was a fan."[20]

Finally, being a Swiftie offers you a chance to find the best people in life: making Swiftie friends is one of the greatest joys. When you meet someone new and tentatively mention that you like Taylor, and it turns out they do too? Unbeatable. Now you can communicate entirely in Taylor lyrics.

However you express your love of Taylor, it has not gone unnoticed. In her letter to the *Wall Street Journal* about the value of music in 2014, Taylor described her relationship with her fans as "a love affair." As she wrote in the secret message encoded in the lyrics to "Mary's

Song (Oh My My My)" on *Taylor Swift*, "Sometimes, love is forever":

> *Some songs and albums represent seasons of our lives, like relationships that we hold dear in our memories but had their time and place in the past. However, some artists will be like finding "the one." We will cherish every album they put out until they retire and we will play their music for our children and grandchildren. As an artist, this is the dream bond we hope to establish with our fans.[21]*

- **"Nobody physically saw me for a year."**
  Use whenever you step away from your phone
  for an hour.

- **"Beautiful gowns."**
  The great Aretha Franklin herself damned
  Taylor with this faint praise in 2014.

- **"In my *rep* era."**
  A wide range of applications for when you want to
  be chaotic.

- **"I would very much like to be excluded from
  this narrative."**
  For when you don't want to go to the event.

- **"Not a lot going on at the moment."**
  This is her *lying*. Say when you do, in fact,
  have a lot going on at the moment.

Mastermind

13

THE GENIUS OF TAYLOR SWIFT

*M*ultiple Album of the Year Grammys. The highest-grossing tour of all time. A species of millipede named *Nannaria swiftae*. A billion dollars in the savings account. Friends with Beyoncé. Do these sound like occurrences that happen to a person by chance?

When it came to writing the final track of *Midnights*, Taylor thought, "Wouldn't it be fun to have a lyric about being calculated? It's something that's been thrown at me like a dagger, but now I take it as a compliment."[1] Earlier in her career, Taylor said she used to bow to pressure to seem sweet and even naive, instead of rightfully claiming responsibility for all her hard work: "I tried very hard—and this is one thing I regret—to convince people that I wasn't the one holding the puppet strings [. . .] I felt for a very long time that people don't want to think of a woman in music who isn't just a happy, talented accident."[2] Now Taylor is proud to say she's a "Mastermind." She's the architect who draws up the plans for her own career.

LAYING THE GROUNDWORK

Staying relevant as a popstar requires fancy footwork. *Midnights*, Taylor's tenth studio album, has sold 3.5 million copies as of 2024, just as conventional wisdom says she should be fading. In just a year, it eclipsed the global sales of *Lover* and came close to equaling those of *reputation*.[3] Numbers are not the whole story, and it's not always useful to compare albums that were released in different years; the market has changed completely since *1989* (10 million global sales and counting) came out, warped by streaming (which contributes toward sales but accounts for less, and pays less, than a vinyl record or digital download) and plays on social media platforms like TikTok. It's also about the passion an artist inspires, the atmosphere they can create in a stadium, and the legacy they shape. Taylor is undoubtedly on a career high, seeing her thirties as her best decade yet.[4] She traveled a long and lonely road to get there. Taylor had been singing live from a young age, taking part in karaoke competitions and singing at any county fair that would let her onstage.[5] She performed the national anthem at a basketball game in 2002, an adorable girl of twelve with apparently perfect self-confidence and a natural love of performing; she told a local newspaper, "I just really love doing that sort of thing. It is an adrenaline rush for me."[6]

Now Taylor is proud to say she's a "Mastermind." She's the architect who draws up the plans for her own career.

Nashville offers a pathway for musicians who can write songs, and a whole machinery ready to snatch you up—if you can find a way in. Taylor figured out that pathway existed by watching TV: "I was watching this special about Faith Hill. It talked about how she went to Nashville. That's the moment that I realized that Nashville's where you need to be if you want to sing country music."[7] Taylor built it up in her head like she was a budding actor with her sights set on Hollywood—she just absolutely had to get there, and she had a plan for how to do it. Nashville's famous Music Row sounds like a great street to get a record deal on—an entire Row dedicated to Music! Taylor and her mother, Andrea, traveled there when Taylor was eleven years old to hand out her demo tapes, which at first included cover versions of other people's songs. Taylor joked that she would walk into reception and hand over her demo, saying, "Hi, I'm Taylor. I'm eleven. I want a record deal, call me."[8] When this didn't work, she realized she needed to show the record companies what made her special.[9] Taylor made a new demo, with self-written songs. One of the first songs Taylor ever wrote was "Lucky You," which shows her pop instincts with classic "do do do do" lyrics. There was also "American Boy," an extremely country song about looking up to your daddy, then growing up and becoming a dad yourself. There were some darker twists in the song, though: the American boy cheats on his "American beauty," and when his kids say they want to be just like him, is that a good or a bad thing?[10]

It's a surprisingly skeptical take on the American dream. The demo was rounded out with a LeAnn Rimes–esque country-rock song called "Smokey Black Nights." Young Taylor arrived in Nashville excited to share her songs with the no doubt equally eager executives. What she found was closed glass doors on the fronts of office buildings. No one was looking to sign an unknown teenage girl to their label: Taylor was told "only thirty-five-year-old house-wives listen to country music and there was no place for a thirteen-year-old on their roster."[11]

Taylor kept working on the skill she would one day describe as "the element of my life that I hold most sacred":[12] songwriting. She used the only method she knew, writing from the heart (and making it catchy). When she next laid siege to Nashville, they saw her potential. Stories about people's rise to fame often skip over the exact details of how they got their chance. In Taylor's case, it was not a lucky chance encounter, it was endless phone calls and striving to persuade record companies to listen to her demo, to hear what she believed the songs could be. Andrea drove her to endless industry showcases, tedious events where a string of singers perform their hearts out in the hope the watching scouts will sign them to a record deal. This eventually worked, and Taylor scored a develop-ment deal with RCA, which Taylor said means "we believe in you—kind of."[13] When this dissolved, Taylor secured a songwriting deal with Sony/ATV Nashville, the youngest person ever to do so, at fourteen years old. She didn't let working with adults intimidate her. Instead, she worked harder, refusing to let her age be a hindrance: "I would come into each meeting with five to ten ideas that were solid. I wanted them to look at me as a person they were writing with, not a little kid."[14] However slowly, the dream was coming true. Taylor's parents were so convinced it was going to happen that they moved the family to Nashville. The next step was to get that record deal.

Taylor's rerecording saga has taught us a lot about music industry finances. When a record company signs an artist, they are placing a bet on them. They advance the money to get the record made, including expensive hours in the studio. The record company's primary motive is to make money. That's why they usually want to own the masters: they paid for them. But many argue that labels should license the copyright from artists rather than owning it outright. In 2005, Taylor eventually signed to Big Machine, a new record label owned by Scott Borchetta. Taylor saw the growth potential: "If I could be a part of building something from the ground up, of being the first artist on a brand-new record label, that would be okay with me as long as I could do something really adventurous and bold and new."[15]

Taylor's Nashville years cemented what was already a strong work ethic: "Country music teaches you to work. You hear stories about these artists who show up four hours late to a photo shoot, and in Nashville that doesn't happen. In Nashville, if you go four hours late to a photo shoot, everyone leaves."[16] It took Taylor's persistence and rare talent, her parents' loving support, time, belief, and financial assistance, and an executive with a vision to get *Taylor Swift* off the ground. All because of an assumption that girls didn't listen to country music, and no one other than teenage girls would ever be interested in Taylor. Women in music endure difficulties on top of the extreme competition and shady contracts that male musicians also face. In 2017, Taylor won a legal case against a DJ who assaulted her by grabbing her bottom—in response to his own case suing *her* for allegedly losing his job over the incident. Taylor described the determined way David Mueller groped her, in front of witnesses and photographers: "He stayed attached to my bare ass-cheek as I lurched away from him."[17] Taylor was one of the world's most famous people and a huge star with a bodyguard standing feet away, and she was still attacked. The jury sided with Taylor and awarded her the symbolic $1 she had asked for. Taylor has said experiences like this are what turned her on to feminism: "The things that happen to you in your life are what develop your political opinions."[18]

When Taylor flexes her bicep onstage during "The Man," she's earned it.

TAYLOR SWIFT IS THE MUSIC INDUSTRY

Taylor always seemed nervous about streaming and its financial model, withholding *Red* from streaming platforms for eight months after releasing it. When *1989* came out, she pulled all her music from Spotify (except for her *evermore*-ish 2012 song "Safe & Sound," a win for fans of The Civil Wars) because it made her music available for free. She explained her reasoning in a letter to the *Wall Street Journal* in 2014: "Music is art, and art is important and rare. Important, rare things are valuable. Valuable things should be paid for. It's my opinion that music should not be free." The letter was stuffed with prescient thoughts, including the role that online followings would begin to hold in creative careers: "For me, this dates back to 2005 when I walked into my first record-label meetings, explaining to them that I had been communicating directly with my fans on this new site called MySpace. In the future, artists will get record deals because they have fans—not the other way around."[19]

A year later, Taylor wrote a (extremely polite) letter to the streaming platform Apple Music, asking that they pay artists more fairly. The platform planned to offer a three-month free trial to new subscribers, during which artists would not be paid for their streams. Taylor seemed concerned she would be belittled for speaking her mind about business: "These are not the complaints of a spoiled, petulant child. These are the echoed sentiments of every artist, writer, and producer in my social circles who are afraid to speak up publicly."[20] Taylor told *Vogue* in 2016 that writing the letter to the all-powerful Apple was the bravest thing she'd ever done.

By 2023, Taylor no longer believed it was overstepping for her to criticize powerful businesses. "The Great War" for Eras Tour tickets in 2022 caused stress to millions: the mere sight of a progress bar can cause raised blood pressure levels in Swifties to this day. Strategies were exchanged, from whether you should refresh the page to what sequence to click the buttons in for maximum chance to secure tickets. In the UK, just registering for the fan presale was a complicated process requiring a code that had been sent out the previous year to people who bought *Midnights*. This was part of a process called Verified Fan, which tries to make sure tickets are sold to real fans and not scalpers who will resell the ticket at an inflated price. A total of 3.5 million people registered, with around 2.4 million fans able to buy tickets.[21] Unfortunately, the presale overwhelmed the system, resulting in the Ticketmaster website crashing and many people being locked out. The public sale was postponed. Taylor was furious, and this time she didn't tread softly to avoid injuring egos:

> [O]ver the years, I've brought so many elements of my career in-house. I've done this SPECIFICALLY to improve the quality of my fans' experience by doing it myself with my team who care as much about my fans as I do. It's really difficult for me to trust an outside entity with these relationships and loyalties, and excruciating for me to just watch mistakes happen with no recourse.[22]

The struggle didn't end with getting tickets; fans also wanted to get to the front of the stadium they'd fought so hard to get access to. Argentinian fans arranged a clever system for gaining access to the open standing area closest to the stage, with fans taking turns to queue, their accumulated hours tracked on a "spreadsheet, created by two organizers and updated by assigned administrators," thus translating into a better place in line.[23] Only Swifties have this level of commitment and spreadsheet abilities, inspired by our head mastermind.

CAPITALISM BARBIE

If we must live in a world where money accumulates in the hands of the few, the way Taylor has made her money is among the least offensive. What's exciting about the story of Taylor's riches is how she self-directed her career, sometimes against the advice of those around her: "A lot of the best things I ever did creatively were things that I

had to really fight—and I mean aggressively fight—to have happen."[24] Billboard estimated that she makes around $536 million a year from music sales, streams, and radio plays. In 2023, she became a billionaire, earning an estimated $1.82 billion from music alone.[25] The impact of this money goes beyond Taylor, because it changes hands for hotel rooms, taxis, trains, and, of course, beads for making bracelets: the *Washington Post* reported that Taylor's six 2023 Eras shows in Los Angeles boosted the local economy by $320 million.[26]

Early in Taylor's career, she made brand deals just like any other celebrity who needed to hustle: the *New Yorker* reported in 2011, "In addition to her perfume [Wonderstruck], she has sold greeting cards, a line of fourteen-dollar Walmart sundresses, Jakks fashion dolls—they wear Swift's outfits and carry mini versions of her Swarovski crystal–encrusted guitar—and, on her website, calendars, iPad skins, Peter Max posters, robes, headbands, journals, and gift bags."[27] Taylor still makes a tidy income from merch (an estimated $2 million at each Eras show), but she has streamlined what she endorses. She can control her own brand, but other brands and people introduce uncertainty. In July 2023, the *New York Times* reported that Taylor had narrowly avoided becoming one of the celebrities who endorsed cryptocurrency to their followers, after failing to agree to a deal for tour sponsorship with a crypto entrepreneur named Sam Bankman-Fried, who has since been convicted of fraud. The *Financial Times* learned that the deal would have included tickets in the form of non-fungible tokens but did not explain what this meant.[28] Swifties have learned many things from Taylor, from the meaning of the word *Machiavellian* to the rules of American football, but this could have been a step too far.

As of 2024, Taylor has never appeared in a campaign for a luxury brand, unlike most of her peers. So far, it hasn't been a good match for her public persona, which, despite everything, still feels like the girl—or, rather, cool, creative woman—next door. Although she wears designer fashion to events, she is also often spotted in less expensive brands that fans are more likely to be able to purchase themselves. In the parlance of celebrity fashion accounts, this means fans can own an "exact"—not a similar item but the exact same one. This is different from influencing because Taylor doesn't endorse the clothes as part of a brand partnership. Instead, the relationship is mutual: brands obviously benefit from their clothes being seen on Taylor, but Taylor also gets to remind us that she's human, and she wears leggings sometimes (there's a limit to how expensive leggings can be). It's useful to Taylor to remain in touch with the financial reality of most fans. Affordability is relative: for some people, a precious piece of Taylor merch is already the most expensive item of clothing in their closet.

Taylor's fashion has its own eras, distinct from the exact looks associated with each album. In her teens, her clothes signaled youth and innocence, as she had to play the part of a role model: "I was a teenager in the public eye at a time when our society was absolutely obsessed with the idea of having perfect young female role models [. . .] if I did slip up, the entire earth would fall off its axis and it would be entirely my fault and I would go to pop-star jail forever and ever."[29] From *Red* to *Lover*, the aim of her red-carpet looks and stage costumes was simple: to broadcast a message to fans about what kind of popstar she was and what kind of music to expect from the new album.

Coming up with a story and expressing it through clothes and hairstyles is one of the most important skills a popstar can have. Taylor's street style often acts as counter-programming to the main narrative: "I had a phase where, for the entirety of 2012, I dressed like a 1950s

From *Red* to *Lover*, the aim of her red-carpet looks and stage costumes was simple: to broadcast a message to fans about what kind of popstar she was and what kind of music to expect from the new album.

housewife."[30] More conservative streetwear soothed the fears of parents and industry folk who were scared that this Taylor who wore shorts onstage might no longer be a "good role model" to children. Taylor wore her first "pants-less" look to the 2014 MTV Video Music Awards; five years earlier, she had arrived at the same event in a Cinderella-inspired horse-drawn carriage and a floor-length gown. An article published the day after she wore the pants-less look in 2014 said the blue playsuit "lets her gorgeous gams do all the sexy work."[31] Coverage like this is well-intentioned and thinks of itself as complimentary, but it shows how quickly the language around a woman can change depending on how many inches of skin she shows.

Taylor hit a messaging peak with her *Lover* aesthetic, which included outfits in acid brights and an array of pastels, clearly ricocheting back to lightness after the black hoodies and burgundy lipstick of *reputation*. The unicorn palette felt like an attempt to lure back kids and families, the clothing equivalent of the notorious spelling-related lyric that was removed from "Me!"[32] Taylor's Technicolor lace-up shorts and canary-yellow T-shirt combination, worn onstage in 2019, was where Taylor's fashion homework showed the most clearly. The outfit feels like an overcorrection to *reputation*. The rainbows nodded to her support for the LGBTQ+ community in "You Need To Calm Down," but ultimately it looked like the costume of a (very expensive) children's party performer. Since 2020, the messages Taylor conveys through her clothes have become more subtle. Her pandemic-era look (flannel shirts, baggy trousers, and self-styled wavy hair) reflected the reality that everyone was wearing elasticated waistbands and hadn't had a haircut since January.

A more sophisticated wardrobe for Taylor emerged in the aftermath, both in terms of the designs she wore and the celebrity subtext that the outfits conveyed. At the premiere of *All Too Well: The Short Film*, which Taylor directed, she wore a deep purple velvet double-breasted suit from the Italian brand Etro (which also made her yellow lace-up *evermore* dress for the Eras Tour). The deep color spoke to adult purpose, a significant change from the pastels of the *Lover* looks. The velvet was rich and textured, and the trim, immaculate cut of the suit expressed Taylor's confidence and creative certainty. Since then, Taylor has worn a sparkling array of outfits with a celestial theme to tie in with *Midnights*. These days, when Taylor wears a certain kind of pretty dress, it is an intentional invisible string back to her teenage years: one of the "Enchanted" gowns on the Eras Tour honors her girlhood, keeping the lilac color and the rhinestone sparkle and turning them up to a spectacular, campy new volume. Offstage, it is still possible to find Easter eggs in Taylor's outfits, especially when she shows up wearing a particular color for days on end, but these days her fashion moments actually feel like they are about fashion.

OUR SONG

Taylor is one of the greatest storytellers of our time. She is a new kind of hero, one who cries as well as flexing her muscles. Taylor has written about vicious conflicts and her moments of deepest despair. She has been the fairy princess, the witch, the good girl, and the bad girl. She's called herself a people-pleaser, a monster, a nightmare, and a daydream. Taylor Swift continuously writes her own story: "My life doesn't gravitate toward being edgy, sexy, or cool. I am just naturally not any of those things. I'm imaginative. I'm smart. And I'm hardworking. Those things are not necessarily prioritized in pop culture."[33]

Taylor used to be seen as two-dimensional. She has now blended the different aspects of her personality together and emerged as someone with inimitable depths, the greatest of these surely yet to be revealed. She says, "Writing songs has never been a strategic element of my career. But I'm not scared anymore to say that other things in my career, like how to market an album, are strictly strategic. And I'm sick of women not being able to say that they have strategic business minds—because male artists are allowed to. And so I'm sick and tired of having to pretend like I don't mastermind my own business. But, it's a different part of my brain than I use to write."[34] Taylor's songwriting will always define her—it is how she achieved her stratospheric level of success, something she has never been afraid to talk about: "There is a false stigma around eagerness in our culture of 'unbothered ambivalence.' This outlook perpetuates the idea that it's not cool to 'want it.' That people who don't try hard are fundamentally more chic than people who do."[35]

Taylor opposes this form of nonchalance by continuously and intentionally using her favorite themes and symbols in her lyrics. It is fun to spot certain colors, objects, and times of day. What began as an evocative detail builds up through repeated mentions into something rich and layered: an icon. It fights the throwaway reputation of pop. It reasserts her as the person in control of the Taylor-Verse: everything there has significance because she says it does. Taylor is a rarity in the way she can remain vulnerable enough to keep making art that we care about while handling her business like a pro and making no apology for it: "Sorry, was I loud? In the house that I bought, with the songs that I wrote, about my own life?"[36]

Taylor has spent her career working to create an imaginative universe that fans would want to spend time inside, from the moonlit lake she pictured in "Tim McGraw" to the stained-glass windows of "Would've, Could've, Should've." She's a planning genius, yes, but she blends this skill with her sensitivity, which she protected even when she had to toughen up: "I want to still have a sharp pen, a thick skin, and an open heart."[37] She's written magic into the rain, gold into the daylight, and sparkles onto the dress she wore once upon a midnight. But what is it, really, that makes her so special?

You could spend your whole life trying to put that into words.

Endnotes

Chapter 1—Origin Story—*Taylor Swift*

1   https://ew.com/article/2008/02/05/taylor-swifts-road-fame/
2   Background: https://www.independent.co.uk/news/long_reads/radio
    -tour-is-not-for-the-weak-inside-the-first-step-to-country-music
    -stardom-a7798561.html
3   https://swiftlegacypodcast.podbean.com/e/the-og-swiftie-holly
    -armstrong/
4   https://www.eonline.com/news/814021/13-things-we-learned-from
    -taylor-swift-s-former-internet-life-on-myspace-youtube-and-more
5   https://www.newstatesman.com/culture/music/2021/04/taylor-swift
    -fearless-version-2008-original-release-fans
6   https://www.rollingstone.com/music/music-news/22-things-you
    -learn-hanging-out-with-taylor-swift-101118/2/
7   https://www.elle.com/culture/music/interviews/a10083/women-in
    -music-taylor-swift-326464/
8   https://ew.com/article/2008/02/05/taylor-swifts-road-fame/
9   https://www.youtube.com/watch?v=UEeWmItgdxA
10 https://www.youtube.com/watch?v=D8i9p8YOxFw
11 Debut-era videos, including "Our Song," were styled by Sandi Spika
    Borchetta, the wife of Taylor's record label boss, Scott Borchetta.
12 https://www.youtube.com/watch?v=D8i9p8YOxFw
13 *Long Pond Sessions*
14 Originally posted on taylorswift.com, captured on fan websites like
    Fanpop.com: https://www.fanpop.com/clubs/taylor-swift/articles
    / 34352/title/behind-song-list-taylors-story-behind-some-songs

Chapter 2—Into the Spotlight—*Fearless*

1   Seth Meyers, former head writer on *Saturday Night Live*, said, "When
    she finished, I should've said, 'Now Taylor, just for you, I want to look at
    you and read what we had written for you just so you know how much
    fucking worse it was. Not only is your song great, but you cannot even
    begin to imagine how shitty what we were doing for you is compared
    to how great what you did for yourself is.'" https://www.hollywood
    reporter.com/tv/tv-news/seth-meyers-praises-taylor-swift-writing
    -own-snl-monologue-1235633986/
2   https://www.theguardian.com/music/2012/oct/18/taylor-swift-want
    -believe-pretty-lies

3   https://people.com/celebrity/taylor-swift-calvin-harris-break-up-her
    -quotes-on-heartbreak-and-moving-on/
4   https://www.npr.org/2012/11/03/164186569/taylor-swift-my
    -confidence-is-easy-to-shake
5   https://www.rollingstone.com/music/music-features/taylor-swift
    -rolling-stone-interview-880794/
6   https://www.vibe.com/features/editorial/taylor-swift-lil-wayne
    -fireman-first-rap-memorized-243115/
7   For example, sampling "Out Of The Woods" on "Question . . .?"
    Checked on https://www.whosampled.com/Taylor-Swift/samples/.
    Most of these are retroactive interpolations and there's a drum sound
    sampled on "London Boy," which hardly counts.
8   https://www.theguardian.com/music/2012/oct/18/taylor-swift-want
    -believe-pretty-lies
9   https://americansongwriter.com/behind-the-meaning-of-taylor
    -swifts-romeo-and-juliet-inspired-love-story/
10 https://www.youtube.com/shorts/_hwt9Oyx7Q8
11 https://www.billboard.com/music/music-news/taylor-swift-zane
    -lowe-beats-1-interview-8541404/
12 *The Morning Call* interview, which is only accessible from the US but
    archived on Americansongwriter.com: https://americansongwriter
    .com/behind-the-meaning-of-taylor-swifts-romeo-and-juliet
    -inspired-love-story/

Chapter 3—The Final Fairy Tale—*Speak Now*

1   *Speak Now (Taylor's Version)* prologue: https://genius.com/Taylor
    -swift-speak-now-taylors-version-prologue-annotated
2   https://www.albionpleiad.com/2010/11/true-life-im-anti-taylor-swift/
3   https://www.reddit.com/media?url=https%3A%2F%2Fi.redd.it%2F
    speak-now-taylors-version-full-prologue-v0-5v75bnxjydab1.jp
    g%3Fs%3D51f5162fe4fb75312a33422c1b18293510f16daf
4   https://www.glamour.com/story/taylor-swift-bomb-shell-in-blue
    -jeans
5   https://www.cp24.com/album-sales-plunge-in-2008-digital
    -downloads-up-1.356342
6   https://www.npr.org/2008/11/28/97583296/hey-has-anybody
    -noticed-that-taylor-swift-cant-sing
7   https://www.billboard.com/music/awards/taylor-swift-woman
    -of-the-decade-speech-billboard-women-in-music-8546156/
8   My fave documentary, on backing singers: *20 Feet From Stardom*
    https://www.imdb.com/title/tt2396566/
9   https://www.youtube.com/watch?v=SqO8a0S8c-8
10 https://www.cosmopolitan.com/entertainment/celebs/a44333575
    /taylor-swift-asked-fans-not-to-cyberbully-john-mayer-dear-john-live/

11 https://twitter.com/taylorswift13/status/1677168840625496065?ref
    _src=twsrc%5Etfw%7Ctwcamp%5Etweetembed%7Ctwter
    m%5E1677168840625496065%7Ctwgr%5E45ca9abbbb776347a6f34d
    5b41e4f7900de35dd4%7Ctwcon%5Es1_&ref_url=https%3A%2F%2Fwww
    .standard.co.uk%2Fnews%2Fworld%2Ftaylor-swift-who-dear-john-last
    -kiss-better-than-revenge-b1092935.html
12 https://www.youtube.com/watch?v=dvmLlM8YXYA
13 https://www.independent.ie/entertainment/music/dont-go-breaking
    -my-heart-taylor-swift-opens-up/30683975.html
14 https://www.theguardian.com/music/2014/aug/23/taylor-swift-shake
    -it-off
15 https://amp.tmz.com/2019/08/21/taylor-swift-plans-rerecord-masters
    -scooter-braun-purchase-big-machine/?_twitter_impression=true
16 https://www.reuters.com/article/idUSTRE69E5RK/
17 https://www.billboard.com/music/music-news/taylor-swift-the-billboard
    -cover-story-953737/
18 Nicole + Felicia also made Taylor's gowns in the video for "I Bet You
    Think About Me." The video's premise echoes "Speak Now":
    Taylor shows up at the wedding of her ex-flame, but in this version
    of events, she rejects him. Throughout the video Taylor wears red,
    except for a white gown she wears to slow dance with her ex.
    Instead of running off with him, she walks away and her gown turns
    red. We see Taylor performing on a stage with her band, playing a
    red guitar.
19 https://twitter.com/SwiftNYC/status/1677882417728610307
20 https://www.refinery29.com/en-gb/2021/04/10414694/taylor-swift
    -change-lyrics-meaning-fearless
21 https://www.youtube.com/watch?v=QboJ2ihbojo
22 Keith Urban is the HATLESS MAN. 2009 CMAs: https://www.youtube
    .com/watch?v=qqYuCosWczE
23 2009 CMAs: https://www.youtube.com/watch?v=qqYuCosWczE
24 https://eu.usatoday.com/story/life/music/2012/10/17/taylor-swift
    -red-interview/1637307/
25 *Rolling Stone Top 500 Greatest Albums of All Time* podcast on *Red*

Chapter 4—I Remember—*Red*

1 https://www.youtube.com/watch?v=SqVxCVblSfA
2 Speaking to Brittany Spanos at *Rolling Stone*: https://www.youtube
   .com/watch?v=4Sn5DbZ4s2Q
3 https://www.youtube.com/watch?v=4Sn5DbZ4s2Q
4 https://www.bbc.co.uk/news/entertainment-arts-67111517
5 https://www.youtube.com/watch?v=IF72ZCWuQpk
6 https://www.rollingstone.com/music/music-news/taylor-swift-diane
   -warren-say-dont-go-thank-you-flowers-1234865606/

7   https://www.theguardian.com/music/2012/oct/18/taylor-swift-want
    -believe-pretty-lies
8   https://www.youtube.com/watch?v=4Sn5DbZ4s2Q
9   https://www.youtube.com/watch?v=4Sn5DbZ4s2Q
10 https://www.youtube.com/watch?v=UEeWmItgdxA
11 https://genius.com/Taylor-swift-last-kiss-lyrics
12 https://time.com/3144645/taylor-swift-shake-it-off-22-pumpkin-spice
    -latte/
13 https://www.buzzfeed.com/chelseamarshall/how-basic-are-you
14 https://www.rollingstone.com/music/music-news/22-things-you
    -learn-hanging-out-with-taylor-swift-101118/
15 https://www.vice.com/en/article/wjvaay/taylor-swifts-kennedy
    -obsession-may-have-inspired-her-4th-of-july-parties
16 https://www.elle.com/culture/celebrities/a43818269/ed-sheeran
    -taylor-swift-friendship/
17 https://www.washingtonpost.com/style/2023/09/20/taylor-swift-vault
    -puzzle-1989-tracks/
18 https://www.rollingstone.com/music/music-news/taylor-swift-hosts
    -red-listening-party-in-new-york-59377/
19 https://www.youtube.com/watch?v=3i4sYbyzsfw
20 https://www.thetimes.co.uk/article/taylor-swift-it-sounds-dorky-but
    -this-is-how-i-write-my-song-lyrics-kmpjksm95
21 https://www.etonline.com/taylor-swift-says-red-scarf-in-all-too-well
    -is-a-metaphor-190595
22 https://www.goodmorningamerica.com/culture/story/taylor-swift
    -turned-story-fans-song-81443975

Chapter 5—New York Streets and Electric Beats—*1989*

1   https://www.billboard.com/music/music-news/taylor-swift-new-york
    -city-welcome-ambassador-6296765/
2   https://www.nme.com/news/music/taylor-swift-199-1241766
3   https://wildest-swift.tumblr.com/post/124453526149/compilation-of
    -taylors-clean-speeches-from-the
4   https://www.elle.com/culture/music/news/a33100/taylor-swift-blank
    -space-grammy-museum/
5   https://www.youtube.com/watch?v=7VenlV7Qxak
6   https://www.billboard.com/music/awards/billboard-woman-of-the
    -year-taylor-swift-on-writing-her-6363514/
7   "Blank Space (voice memo)"
8   https://www.youtube.com/watch?v=7VenlV7Qxak
9   https://www.rollingstone.com/music/music-news/the-reinvention
    -of-taylor-swift-116925/

10 https://www.wsj.com/articles/for-taylor-swift-the-future-of-music
-is-a-love-story-1404763219
11 https://www.wonderlandmagazine.com/2014/11/17/cover-story-taylor-swift/
12 https://www.rollingstone.com/music/music-news/the-reinvention
-of-taylor-swift-116925/4/
13 https://www.youtube.com/watch?v=7VenlV7Qxak
14 https://www.maxim.com/entertainment/taylor-swift-tops-2015
-maxim-hot-100/
15 https://www.youtube.com/watch?v=7VenlV7Qxak
16 https://www.npr.org/2014/10/31/359827368/anything-that-connects
-a-conversation-with-taylor-swift

Chapter 6—Snakes and Ladders—*reputation*

1 https://www.vogue.com/article/taylor-swift-may-cover-maid-of-honor
-dating-personal-style
2 https://time.com/6342806/person-of-the-year-2023-taylor-swift/
3 https://www.musicradar.com/news/taylor-swift-getaway-car-bridge
4 *Miss Americana*
5 https://www.youtube.com/watch?v=wl44s5xZl0E&t=17s
6 https://www.capitalfm.com/artists/taylor-swift/news/strong-female-friends/
7 Ibid.
8 *Miss Americana*
9 https://time.com/6342806/person-of-the-year-2023-taylor-swift/
10 Ibid.
11 https://www.wsj.com/articles/for-taylor-swift-the-future-of-music-is
-a-love-story-1404763219
12 *Miss Americana*
13 https://www.rollingstone.com/music/music-features/taylor-swift
-rolling-stone-interview-880794/
14 https://www.youtube.com/watch?v=VA7Y_Psp5l4
15 https://www.rollingstone.co.uk/music/features/call-it-what-you-want
-a-full-timeline-of-taylor-swift-and-joe-alwyns-relationship-28366/
16 https://www.businessinsider.com/taylor-swift-lover-diary-entries
-about-kanye-west-joe-alwyn-2019-8?r=US&IR=T
17 Ibid.
18 https://www.teenvogue.com/story/taylor-swift-fans-dress-parents
19 https://people.com/music/taylor-swift-brother-austin-favorite
-reputation-song/
20 https://www.vogue.com/article/taylor-swift-cover-september-2019
21 https://www.youtube.com/watch?v=gHG-tdupKHQ
22 "It was a big goal of mine": https://www.rollingstone.com/music/music
-news/22-things-you-learn-hanging-out-with-taylor-swift-101118/

Chapter 7—What Really Matters—*Lover*

1 *Reputation Stadium Tour*
2 https://www.elle.com/culture/celebrities/a26628467/taylor-swift-30th -birthday-lessons/
3 https://www.youtube.com/watch?v=dDO6HnY7h24
4 https://www.elle.com/culture/celebrities/a26628467/taylor-swift-30th -birthday-lessons/
5 https://www.instagram.com/p/B2hAlecjv5J/
6 https://dailytargum.com/article/2019/10/taylor-swift-lover-review
7 https://variety.com/2020/music/features/taylor-swift-politics-sundance -documentary-miss-americana-1203471910/
8 Ibid.
9 https://www.vulture.com/article/taylor-swift-rerecorded-albums -which-album-is-next.html
10 https://www.vogue.com/article/taylor-swift-cover-september-2019
11 https://www.youtube.com/watch?app=desktop&v=2AUUnLixsFQ
12 https://www.rollingstone.com/music/music-news/taylor-swift-kelly -clarkson-sends-flowers-recording-1234874502/
13 https://time.com/6342806/person-of-the-year-2023-taylor-swift/
14 https://www.vox.com/culture/2016/11/8/13565144/who-is-taylor-swift -voting-for-clinton-trump-election
15 https://www.theguardian.com/music/2019/aug/24/taylor-swift -pop-music-hunger-games-gladiators
16 https://www.rollingstone.com/music/music-features/the-liberation -of-kesha-123984/
17 https://www.elle.com/culture/celebrities/a26628467/taylor-swift-30th -birthday-lessons/
18 https://time.com/4667037/katy-perry-single-chained-to-the-rhythm/; https://www.forbes.com/sites/hughmcintyre/2017/03/16/is-katy-perrys -new-song-chained-to-the-rhythm-a-flop/
19 https://www.elle.com/culture/celebrities/a26628467/taylor-swift-30th -birthday-lessons/
20 *Miss Americana*
21 https://slate.com/culture/2023/10/cruel-summer-number-1-taylor-swift -billboard.html
22 https://taylorswiftstyle.com/post/99180839912
23 https://people.com/pets/taylor-swift-tells-fans-cat-meredith-isnt -missing-just-private/
24 https://twitter.com/taylorswift13/status/1239670332958674944?lang=en
25 https://www.rollingstone.com/music/music-news/the-reinvention-of -taylor-swift-116925/2/
26 *Lover* Instagram live
27 *Long Pond Sessions*
28 https://time.com/5577508/taylor-swift-influences-cats-tumblr/

29   https://www.latimes.com/entertainment-arts/movies/story/2019-10
     -30/taylor-swift-cats-andrew-lloyd-webber
30   https://variety.com/2020/music/features/taylor-swift-politics-sundance
     -documentary-miss-americana-1203471910/
31   https://www.youtube.com/watch?time_continue=28&v=o7EG4UHaok
     8&embeds_referring_euri=https%3A%2F%2Ftaylorswiftswitzerland
     .ch%2F&embeds_referring_origin=https%3A%2F%2Ftaylorswift
     switzerland.ch&source_ve_path=Mjg2NjY&feature=emb_logo
32   https://www.youtube.com/watch?v=TC1UnBDfrQA
33   https://www.rollingstone.com/music/music-features/taylor-swift-rolling
     -stone-interview-880794/
34   https://variety.com/2020/music/features/taylor-swift-politics-sundance
     -documentary-miss-americana-1203471910/

Chapter 8—Into the Woods—*folklore*

1   Taylor Swift's Songwriting Process on 'evermore' | Apple Music: https://
     www.youtube.com/watch?v=CQacWbsLbS4&t=27s
2   https://www.nme.com/news/music/read-taylor-swift-new-personal
     -essay-explaining-eighth-album-folklore-2714540
3   *Long Pond Sessions*
4   Ibid.
5   https://www.rollingstone.com/music/music-features/taylor-swift-rolling
     -stone-interview-880794/
6   This sounds impossible, but Justin Bieber's *Journals* (2014), a passion
     project with an R&B sound, neither enhanced nor derailed his pop
     career. Without a big hit or promotional campaign, it's like it doesn't
     exist outside of his dedicated fandom.
7   Taylor Swift's Songwriting Process on 'evermore' | Apple Music: https://
     www.youtube.com/watch?v=CQacWbsLbS4&t=27s
8   *Long Pond Sessions*
9   https://ew.com/music/taylor-swift-entertainers-of-the-year-2020/
10   *Long Pond Sessions*
11   https://www.vogue.com/article/taylor-swift-cover-september-2019
12   *Long Pond Sessions*
13   Ibid.
14   Taylor Swift's Songwriting Process on 'evermore' | Apple Music: https://
     www.youtube.com/watch?v=CQacWbsLbS4&t=27s
15   *Long Pond Sessions*
16   The name James in the song has been interpreted as both male and
     female: Taylor's close friend Blake Lively has a daughter named James.
     Taylor's own name was chosen due to its gender-neutral nature. How-
     ever, Taylor stated in the *Long Pond Sessions* that James is a teenage
     boy, and the song was written from a masculine perspective.
17   *Long Pond Sessions*

18   https://www.vogue.com/article/taylor-swift-cover-september-2019
19   Source: original research, 2024
20   *Long Pond Sessions*
21   Taylor Swift's Songwriting Process on 'evermore' | Apple Music: https://
      www.youtube.com/watch?v=CQacWbsLbS4&t=27s
22   *Long Pond Sessions*
23   Ibid.
24   https://americansongwriter.com/behind-the-introspective-meaning
      -of-mirrorball-by-taylor-swift/
25   *Long Pond Sessions*
26   *Ibid.*
27   Onstage at the Eras Tour
28   https://variety.com/vip/the-power-of-tiktok-on-taylor-swift-eras-tour
      -1235752739/

Chapter 9—The Graveyard Shift—*evermore*

1   *Miss Americana*
2   Taylor Swift's Songwriting Process on 'evermore' | Apple Music: https://
     www.youtube.com/watch?v=CQacWbsLbS4&t=27s
3   https://www.popbuzz.com/music/artists/taylor-swift/news/willow
     -written-10-minutes-aaron-dessner/
4   https://web.archive.org/web/20200322105433/https://www.youtube
     .com/watch?v=vtQC8ILxHCs
5   Second was *Pet Sounds* by the Beach Boys, first was *What's Going On*
     by Marvin Gaye: https://www.rollingstone.com/music/music-lists
     /best-albums-of-all-time-1062063/marvin-gaye-whats-going-on
     -4-1063232/
6   https://jonimitchell.com/library/view.cfm?id=2962
7   https://jonimitchell.com/library/view.cfm?id=2313
8   https://www.theguardian.com/music/2012/oct/18/taylor-swift-want
     -believe-pretty-lies
9   Taylor Swift's Songwriting Process on 'evermore' | Apple Music: https://
     www.youtube.com/watch?v=CQacWbsLbS4&t=27s: "tolerate it also
     contains a lot of subtext, when Taylor sings about painting her lover's
     portrait using her best paints. Like Betty talking about James on "cardi-
     gan" from *folklore*, Taylor's mostly flattering pen portraits of past loves
     give them a romance they haven't necessarily earned.
10   *Folklore: The Long Pond Studio Sessions*
11   Hotly debated in the time signatures community but confirmed by
     Aaron Dessner in *Rolling Stone*: https://www.rollingstone.com/music
     /music-features/aaron-dessner-interview-taylor-swift-evermore
     -1105853/
12   The eight seconds of white noise went to number one on the Canadian
     iTunes chart in 2014.

13   https://www.rollingstone.com/music/music-news/22-things-you-learn
     -hanging-out-with-taylor-swift-101118/
14   Ibid.
15   https://time.com/3578249/taylor-swift-interview/
16   "Taylor Swift's Songwriting Process on 'evermore' | Apple Music:
     https://www.youtube.com/watch?v=CQacWbsLbS4&t=27s"
17   Ibid.
18   https://www.rollingstone.com/music/music-features/aaron-dessner
     -interview-taylor-swift-evermore-1105853/
19   Taylor Swift's Songwriting Process on 'evermore' | Apple Music: https://
     www.youtube.com/watch?v=CQacWbsLbS4&t=27s
20   Ibid.
21   https://www.billboard.com/music/country/taylor-swift-nashville
     -songwriter-awards-full-speech-1235142144/
22   Ibid.
23   Taylor Swift's Songwriting Process on 'evermore' | Apple Music: https://
     www.youtube.com/watch?v=CQacWbsLbS4&t=27s
24   For a clear example, listen to Hank Williams's "I'm So Lonesome I Could
     Cry" (1949).
25   Excerpt from "After great pain, a formal feeling comes—" (c.1862)

Chapter 10—The Stars Align—*Midnights*

1   Taylor Swift's Songwriting Process on 'evermore' | Apple Music: https://
    www.youtube.com/watch?v=CQacWbsLbS4&t=27s
2   https://time.com/6342806/person-of-the-year-2023-taylor-swift/
3   https://www.youtube.com/watch?v=UEeWmItgdxA
4   Nothing.
5   https://www.thelineofbestfit.com/news/taylor-swift-shares-midnights
    -album-promo-schedule-and-teases-special-very-chaotic-surprise
6   *The Graham Norton Show*
7   Aaron Dessner worked on songs from the extended "3 a.m. edition"
    of *Midnights*: "Hits Different," "The Great War," "High Infidelity," and
    "Would've, Could've, Should've."
8   Other recent recipients of the Country Music Awards Song of the Year
    honor have included "Fast Car" by Tracy Chapman in 2023 (following the
    success of the cover version by Luke Combs), making her the first Black re-
    cipient of the award; and "Girl Crush" in 2015, also performed by Little Big
    Town and cowritten by Liz Rose, Taylor's writing partner on "All Too Well."
9   https://www.rollingstone.com/music/music-news/kelly-clarkson-taylor
    -swift-better-man-taylors-version-1234666210/
10 https://www.cbsnews.com/newyork/news/taylor-swift-says-red-has-a
    -song-for-every-emotion/
11 https://ohnotheydidnt.livejournal.com/92069741.html?page=4
12 https://www.youtube.com/watch?v=jkWL7_fNR7E

13   "Love Story" was held off the number one slot by Kelly Clarkson's "My Life Would Suck Without You," written and produced by Max Martin.

14   Source for stats: https://www.officialcharts.com/charts/singles-chart /20090301/7501/

15   https://www.buzzfeednews.com/article/beimengfu/theres-a-new -blank-space-in-chinese-wallets

16   International Federation of the Phonographic Industry

17   *Wonderland* magazine, November 2014. This shoot suggests a parallel Taylor-Verse where she looks like a 1980s girl-band member, with a wet-look quiff.

18   https://www.npr.org/2012/11/03/164186569/taylor-swift-my-confidence -is-easy-to-shake

19   https://www.buzzfeed.com/elliewoodward/you-make-me-so-happy -it-turns-back-to-sad

20   https://www.rollingstone.com/music/music-features/aaron-dessner -interview-taylor-swift-evermore-1105853/

21   https://www.billboard.com/music/music-news/taylor-swift-nyu -commencement-speech-full-transcript-1235072824/

22   https://www.elle.com/culture/celebrities/a26628467/taylor-swift-30th -birthday-lessons/

23   https://www.instagram.com/p/Cj9ir4EOrL4/?hl=en

24   https://variety.com/2020/music/news/taylor-swift-eating-disorder -netflix-documentary-miss-americana-1203478047/

25   https://www.rollingstone.com/music/music-news/the-reinvention -of-taylor-swift-116925/4/

26   https://www.elle.com/culture/celebrities/a26628467/taylor-swift-30th -birthday-lessons/

27   https://www.billboard.com/music/music-news/taylor-swift-nyu -commencement-speech-full-transcript-1235072824/

28   "All Too Well (10 Minute Version) (Taylor's Version) (From The Vault)"

29   https://www.elle.com/culture/celebrities/a26628467/taylor-swift-30th -birthday-lessons/

30   Ibid.

31   "If you don't look back at pictures of some of your old looks and cringe, you're doing it wrong. See: Bleachella": https://www.elle.com/culture /celebrities/a26628467/taylor-swift-30th-birthday-lessons/

32   "Taylor Swift puts ice cubes in her wine—but do experts believe this ruins it?": https://www.express.co.uk/celebrity-news/1822276/Taylor -Swift-ice-cubes-white-wine-tips

Chapter 11—Spinning in Her Best Dress: Taylor on Tour

1   https://www.youtube.com/watch?v=XarVd2TSmqI&t=204s

2   https://mb.com.ph/2023/3/21/taylor-swift-breaks-madonna-s-concert -attendance-record-1#google_vignette

3   https://tasteofcountry.com/taylor-swift-diary-entry-2006-rascal-flatts
      -tour/?utm_source=tsmclip&utm_medium=referral
4   https://countryfancast.com/eric-church-and-rascal-flatts/
5   https://globalgrind.com/4033001/taylor-swift-time-magazine-cover
      -photos-interview/
6   https://www.theguardian.com/music/2014/aug/23/taylor-swift-shake
      -it-off
7   *Journey to Fearless*
8   Ibid.
9   https://time.com/3583129/power-of-taylor-swift-cover/
10   Source: I was there.
11   https://www.youtube.com/watch?v=CL4eoy9ywic
12   https://time.com/3578249/taylor-swift-interview/
13   https://time.com/3583129/power-of-taylor-swift-cover/
14   *Speak Now World Tour Live*
15   https://www.dailymail.co.uk/femail/article-2684013/Swifts-love-advice
      -music-industry.html
16   Reputation Tour https://www.youtube.com/watch?v=uqGqWJhu668
17   https://ew.com/music/2019/05/09/taylor-swift-cover-story/
18   https://time.com/6343028/taylor-swift-workout-routine-eras-tour/
19   *Long Pond Sessions*
20   https://time.com/6342806/person-of-the-year-2023-taylor-swift/

Chapter 12—A People's History of Taylor Swift: The Fans

1   https://nypost.com/2023/12/28/business/taylor-swift-brings-vinyl
      -record-sales-to-new-heights/
2   Ibid.
3   https://people.com/taylor-swift-the-eras-tour-concert-film
      -everything-to-know-tickets-runtime-7964229
4   Manila is the city that carries out the most searches for "Taylor Swift,"
      according to 2023 Google statistics.
5   https://www.youtube.com/watch?v=MduXSkFvaO4
6   https://www.cosmopolitan.com/entertainment/celebs/a43488940
      /taylor-swift-surprised-fan-viral-tiktok-dance-bejeweled-eras-tour/
7   https://www.youtube.com/watch?v=G9I8ua1EcW4
8   https://www.tumblr.com/alltoooooowell/628909213615292416/taylor
      -swift-and-easter-eggs
9   https://www.youtube.com/watch?v=O3YGh73XQU8
10   Ibid.
11   Ibid.
12   Ibid.
13   https://pitchfork.com/reviews/albums/21101-1989/
14   "What did the five holes mean? Were they counting down to some-
      thing? Was she trying to tell us something about the fence?"

15   https://twitter.com/taylorswift13/status/1163118375607963648?lang=en
16   https://www.rollingstone.com/music/music-features/taylor-swift
      -rolling-stone-interview-880794/
17   https://www.today.com/popculture/music/taylor-swift-sexuality
      -rcna122455
18   https://www.nytimes.com/2024/01/04/opinion/taylor-swift-queer.
      html?searchResultPosition=4
19   https://www.washingtonpost.com/entertainment/2023/12/26/taylor
      -swift-eras-conference-academic/
20   https://www.washingtonpost.com/style/of-interest/2023/10/20/taylor
      -swift-fandom-eras-tour/
21   https://www.wsj.com/articles/for-taylor-swift-the-future-of-music-is
      -a-love-story-1404763219

Chapter 13—Mastermind: The Genius of Taylor Swift

1   https://time.com/6342806/person-of-the-year-2023-taylor-swift/
2   https://www.rollingstone.com/music/music-features/taylor-swift
     -rolling-stone-interview-880794/
3   https://chartmasters.org/taylor-swift-albums-and-songs-sales
     /#taylor_swifts_album_sales
4   https://time.com/6342806/person-of-the-year-2023-taylor-swift/
5   https://www.salon.com/2015/05/22/taylor_swift_is_not_an_underdog
     _the_real_story_about_her_1_percent_upbringing_that_the_new
     _york_times_wont_tell_you/
6   https://www.youtube.com/watch?v=6E63AeaHczE (newspaper is
     screenshotted at the end)
7   https://www.youtube.com/watch?v=XarVd2TSmqI&t=204s
8   Ibid.
9   *Journey to Fearless*
10   https://genius.com/Taylor-swift-american-boy-lyrics
11   https://www.billboard.com/music/music-news/taylor-swift-nyu
     -commencement-speech-full-transcript-1235072824/
12   https://www.nytimes.com/2019/12/24/arts/music/taylor-swift-lover
     .html
13   https://www.youtube.com/watch?v=vnIZN0WgrAE
14   https://www.nytimes.com/2008/11/09/arts/music/09cara.html
15   *Journey to Fearless*
16   https://www.esquire.com/entertainment/music/a30491/taylor
     -swift-1114/
17   https://www.washingtonpost.com/news/arts-and-entertainment/wp
     /2017/12/06/taylor-swift-explains-her-blunt-testimony-during
     -her-sexual-assault-trial/
18   https://www.theguardian.com/music/2019/aug/24/taylor-swift-pop
     -music-hunger-games-gladiators

ENDNOTES

19 https://www.wsj.com/articles/for-taylor-swift-the-future-of-music-is
    -a-love-story-1404763219
20 https://www.stereogum.com/1810310/read-taylor-swifts-open-letter
    -to-apple-music/news/
21 https://business.ticketmaster.com/business-solutions/taylor-swift-the
    -eras-tour-onsale-explained/
22 https://variety.com/2022/music/news/taylor-swift-addresses-eras
    -tour-ticketmaster-fiasco-1235436036/
23 https://pitchfork.com/thepitch/meet-the-argentine-taylor-swift-fans
    -who-have-been-camping-out-for-the-eras-tour-since-june/
24 https://www.rollingstone.com/music/music-features/taylor-swift
    -rolling-stone-interview-880794/
25 https://www.billboard.com/business/business-news/taylor-swift
    -earned-2-billion-music-movie-touring-1235555994/
26 https://www.washingtonpost.com/business/2023/10/13/taylor-swift
    -eras-tour-money-jobs/
27 https://www.newyorker.com/magazine/2011/10/10/taylor-swift-profile
    -you-belong-with-me
28 https://www.ft.com/content/2b0601e2-d371-404d-8531-227f11d4a83f
29 https://www.billboard.com/music/music-news/taylor-swift-nyu
    -commencement-speech-full-transcript-1235072824/
30 Ibid.
31 https://www.eonline.com/news/572353/taylor-swift-ditches-pants
    -wears-short-jumpsuit-for-her-red-carpet-arrival-to-the-2014-mtv
    -music-video-awards
32 https://www.rollingstone.com/music/music-news/taylor-swift-removes
    -me-lyric-874631/
33 https://www.youtube.com/watch?v=0l4fPZ2TmsI
34 https://www.rollingstone.com/music/music-features/taylor-swift
    -rolling-stone-interview-880794/
35 https://www.billboard.com/music/music-news/taylor-swift-nyu
    -commencement-speech-full-transcript-1235072824/
36 *Miss Americana*
37 Ibid.

Acknowledgments

All my thanks to my agent, Maddalena Cavaciuti. I had the time of my life reading contracts with you.

Thank you to my hardworking and brilliant editors, Nicole Witmer and Stephanie Duncan, and to Jennifer Porter and Isabella Ghaffari-Parker at Transworld, all of whom made writing this book really fun as well as a dream come true. My thanks to Maddalena Carrai for the illustrations, Bobby Birchall for the design, and the copy-editing team who all worked so hard to make this book the best it could be.

Thank you to my Swifties, Arielle Steele, Kate Leaver, and Natasha Lunn, for whom no level of Taylor chat is too much. Forever thank you to my friend Jenny Lane-Smith. I am indebted to Beth Davies for providing the call to adventure. My writing group, Afy Nourallah, Gina Killick, Helen Saunders, Nancy Howell, and Kelsey O'Brien, empowered me to write about topics I really cared about; thank you for your patience when this resulted in so much writing on Taylor Swift. Thank you to Billy Payne and Mensa Ansah for music advice. Moral support for this book was provided by Philippa Mander, Sally Mumby-Croft, Katie Weatherall, and Henry Setter. To everyone who has ever engaged in a detailed conversation with me about popstars, thank you—that's how I learned to write this book.

Thank you to my parents, Sipi Hämeenaho and Dominic Fox, and my brother, Oscar Hämeenaho-Fox, for believing in me and reading all my emails. Best family.

Inspirations and Influences

About the Author

Satu Hämeenaho-Fox is a *Fearless*-era Swiftie and author of books about culture. She has written books about many people whose artistry and/or clothes she likes, including Taylor Swift, Harry Styles, Zendaya, and Lady Gaga. She has also written several children's books on art and fashion history for New York's Metropolitan Museum of Art. She is the cofounder of the *Swiftian Theory* newsletter.